LIES AND EPIPHANIES

CHRIS WALTON

LIES AND EPIPHANIES

COMPOSERS AND THEIR INSPIRATION FROM WAGNER TO BERG

UNIVERSITY OF ROCHESTER PRESS

First published 2014

University of Rochester Press
668 Mt. Hope Avenue, Rochester, NY 14620, USA
www.urpress.com
and Boydell & Brewer Limited
PO Box 9, Woodbridge, Suffolk IP12 3DF, UK
www.boydellandbrewer.com

ISBN-13: 978-1-58046-477-2
ISSN: 1071-9989

Library of Congress Cataloging-in-Publication Data

Walton, Chris, 1963– author.
    Lies and epiphanies : composers and their inspiration from Wagner to Berg /
Chris Walton.
        pages cm — (Eastman studies in music, ISSN 1071-9989 ; v. 111)
    Includes bibliographical references and index.
    ISBN 978-1-58046-477-2 (hardcover : alkaline paper) 1. Composition (Music)
2. Composers. 3. Inspiration. 4. Creation (Literary, artistic, etc.) I. Title.
II. Series: Eastman studies in music ; v. 111.
    ML430.W35 2014
    781.3'111—dc23

                                                                    2014003436

A catalogue record for this title is available from the British Library.

This publication is printed on acid-free paper.
Printed in the United States of America.

For Vreni and Martin Germann

CONTENTS

ACKNOWLEDGMENTS

This book has its origins in my research into Mahler's Second Symphony, to which I was prompted by Peter Quantrill. In writing it, I have been aided by numerous other friends and colleagues, in particular Heiri Aerni, Stefan Dell'Olivo, Daniel Gloor, and Alice Robinson of the Zentralbibliothek Zürich; Régine Bonnefoit and Hermann Köstler of the Fondation Oskar Kokoschka; Karin auf der Maur-Reichmuth and Katja Fleischer of the Richard Wagner Museum Luzern; Thomas Leibnitz and Peter Prokop of the Austrian National Library; Jürgen Neubacher of the Hamburg University Library; Nele Tincheva and Michaela Giesing of the Theatersammlung of Hamburg University; Nancy M. Shawcross and John Pollack of the University of Pennsylvania Library; Alex Ross, who pointed my interest in many different directions; and Roger Allen, Antony Beaumont, Wolfgang Gartzke, Martin Germann, Renate Gygax, Stephen E. Hefling, Ray Holden, Tim Jackson, Douglas Jarman, Anna-Barbara Rothen, Gerhard Splitt, and Marie-Pierre and Pierre Walliser. John Tyrrell kindly helped with translations from the Czech of Josef Foerster; Sandro Balzarini helped with setting the music examples; and Isobel Rycroft's aid in procuring various source materials was invaluable. I owe many thanks, too, to the staff of the music library at the Musikhochschule Basel and of the music department of the Zentralbibliothek Solothurn. Hans Müller provided a regular stream of relevant literature that I would otherwise never have found. And from my colleagues at Syntax AG in Zurich—especially Barbara Bruppacher and Sonia Dreiser—I have profited more in my daily work with language(s) than they can suspect.

Much in the chapter on Wagner I owe to Thomas Rösner's interpretations of the composer's music, including the finest performance of the *Siegfried Idyll* I have yet heard; our conversations on Berg and others also helped me to hone the ideas formulated in the chapter on that composer. I am grateful to Antony Bye, the editor of the *Musical Times*, for permission to use some material on Berg and Furtwängler that I originally published in that journal.

Chris Walton
Michaelmas 2013

INTRODUCTION

"Sustaining inspiration will continue to produce a result as good as . . . [here the manuscript breaks off]"

"So if one asks about maintaining inspiration, one is justified inasmuch as . . . [here the manuscript breaks off]"

—From Arnold Schoenberg, "Inspiration," late 1926

G iven the importance that Schoenberg placed on the notion of inspiration, it is ironic that he found this topic so awkward to discuss. He was on other occasions more cogent and less fragmentary than in the sentences quoted above,[1] but his hesitation here serves to remind us that "inspiration" is a concept as vague and difficult to define as it is widely used. Yet it is also a concept as old as the arts to which it supposedly gives birth. Inspiration was to Plato the origin of poetry, and artistic creation itself a kind of divine possession, mysterious and extrarational. In the pre–Enlightenment West, while musical invention was considered to be largely a rational craft that could be learned (an *ars inveniendi*) along with the basics of harmony and counterpoint, the extrarational element—the "divine spark"—never disappeared from the discourse. In the nineteenth century, the source of inspiration was relocated away from the Deity into the subconscious of the composer (even before the concept of the "subconscious" became current) and was a matter of intense fascination to the romantics. Richard Wagner's many ponderings on the topic, derived in part from his favorite philosopher, Arthur Schopenhauer, acquired immense significance for the generations that followed him. Particularly influential were his descriptions of inspirational "visions," such as the opening of his *Rheingold*, purportedly experienced during a state of half-sleep in La Spezia, and *Parsifal*, which came upon him, he claimed, one Good Friday morning in Zurich.

From the late nineteenth century onward, prompted in large part by Wagner, the concept of the *Einfall* was heatedly debated in the German-speaking world. For most composers and commentators (even Hans Pfitzner and Alban Berg, who otherwise seldom agreed on anything), the *Einfall* signified both the moment of inspiration itself and the motif or melody that is its actual product. As the arch-Wagnerian Thomas Mann once noted, it was "a recent musical category. The seventeenth and early eighteenth centuries knew as little of it as they knew of the rights of ownership to particular melodies."[2]

The first notable post-Wagnerian investigation into inspiration was by Friedrich von Hausegger (1837–99), a committed Wagnerite of moderate tone and scholarly method, unlike many who came after him. In the mid-1890s he sent a questionnaire to several German-speaking artists (mostly composers, but also including the painter Max Liebermann and the poet Otto Julius Bierbaum), requesting that they explain their process of artistic creation. He asked specifically whether they had dreams (creative or otherwise), whether matters of "desire" [*Begehren*] had an impact on their creativity, how they would describe their mental state both when the urge to create was present and when it was absent, and so on.[3] He received replies from some of the most prominent men of the day, such as Richard Strauss, Felix Weingartner, Wilhelm Kienzl, and Ernst Niklaus von Reznicek. Strauss and Humperdinck found nature conducive to inspiration, while Bierbaum needed to be near a city but not in it. Kienzl rejected external stimuli such as alcohol, tobacco, and coffee, whereas Humperdinck received the idea for one of his biggest Catholic choral works in the beer-sodden, glass-clunking Hofbräuhaus in Munich. Strauss claimed to have found melodic inspiration from reading Schopenhauer and Nietzsche. Humperdinck compared creation to a dreamlike state; so did Weingartner, who found inspiration in his actual dreams, too.

As a brief survey of composer's attitudes to composition, Hausegger's work is fascinating, and its anecdotal character is a prime source of that fascination. He draws no overall conclusions, though the one matter that becomes clear is that none of his interviewees doubted the importance of the *Einfall*, which could come either in a sudden burst, as in the composition of songs (Strauss) and the overture to an opera (Reznicek's *Donna Diana*), or in less urgent fashion. The possession of a solid technique did not diminish a composer's belief in the *Einfall*.

After the First World War, the composer Hans Pfitzner emerged as the principal, self-appointed guardian of what he perceived as the ideals of Schopenhauer and Wagner, especially in matters of inspiration. He had already made a name for himself as something of a polemicist with his *Futuristengefahr* (The danger of the futurists) of 1917, a reply to the supposedly modernist, un-German dangers posed by Ferruccio Busoni's little tract "A New Aesthetic of Music," which had been published in its second edition in 1916. Next it was the critic Paul Bekker who raised Pfitzner's ire. He had written a study of Beethoven just before the war, in which he had postulated that "the poetic idea" lay behind much of the man's music. Bekker followed this study with several newspaper articles in a similar vein in the ensuing years. By the end of the decade Pfitzner could contain himself no longer at what he felt to be a prolonged attack on the essence of music itself. He published a reply in book form in 1920, its pseudo-Busonian title stressing both the continuity of his opinions and the supposed unity of those whom he saw as the enemies of German art: *Die neue Aesthetik der musikalischen Impotenz: Ein Verwesungssymptom?* (The new aesthetic of musical impotence: A symptom of decay?). In it he accused Bekker of being "amateurish"[4] and denounced his ideas of Beethoven's poeticism, insisting instead that "composing is composing and poetry is poetry!"[5] After a long discussion of Schopenhauer's ideas (and with reference to Plato, too), Pfitzner explains that the crux of music lies in "the one, inexpressible thing that only *it* has: the musical *Einfall* of genius."[6] Pfitzner was convinced that Bekker and others like him were ignoring the mystery of inspiration in favor of a utilitarian view in which rational *gestalten* ("construction," the act of "forming") was supposedly the key to understanding music.[7] "Inspiration is the essence of music as a creative art," he wrote.[8] "The realm of the artistic . . . begins at the point where art cannot be explained and translated for the intellect, but has to be directly viewed and felt."[9]

Pfitzner's little book prompted various ripostes, including one in the journal *Musikblätter des Anbruch* from Alban Berg (at the time a virtual unknown). It was primarily Pfitzner's antimodern stance that enraged Berg, who, while taking issue with Pfitzner's opposition to any kind of analysis, nevertheless insisted that modern music had also produced its fair share of inspired creations (he mentions in this regard the second theme from Schoenberg's Chamber Symphony no. 1).[10] The first edition of Pfitzner's book was peppered with anti-Semitic asides, but a long foreword that he added to its third edition in 1926 verged on the rabid. He now lumped together Alban Berg (without mentioning him by name), Jewishness, the foxtrot, atonality, jazz, circus music, and Americanism as threats to everything truly German and to the mystery of inspiration (which by now he regarded as more or less synonymous with each other and with his own art).[11]

That same year, 1926, the musicologist Arnold Schering published an article—"Geschichtliches zur 'ars inveniendi' in der Musik" (Historical issues pertaining to the "ars inveniendi" in music)—that was in part another reply to Pfitzner (it mentions Pfitzner's battle with Bekker in its first sentence). It aimed to balance out the competing claims, as Schering saw them, of *Erfindung* and *gestalten*, thus of invention (here clearly meaning the inspired *Einfall*) and construction. Schering drew on sources from Glareanus to Mattheson and Sulzer in order to demonstrate, in measured prose, how the art of musical form and construction was in former times regarded by some as of greater significance than the "mere" invention of a theme[12]—a theme could be devised by formulaic means, but the molding of such a theme into a coherent, satisfying work of art required true ability. Schering situates the shift from *Affektenlehre* to a more modern conception that valued *Erfindung* above *gestalten* in the second half of the eighteenth century, citing Beethoven as a prime example of the new direction in music. Schering uses Beethoven's sketchbooks to illustrate how a composer might receive "inspiration" and then proceed through the act of *gestalten* to create great works of art.

In the 1930s, the most notable research on the topic of musical inspiration was carried out by one Julius Bahle, and published as *Der musikalische Schaffensprozess: Psychologie der schöpferischen Erlebnis- und Antriebsformen* in 1936 (The musical process of creation: A psychology of the creative forms of experience and stimulus). In 1931, he sent eight different poems to a series of composers, requesting them to set one to music and asking them—like Hausegger nearly four decades before—to document their process of composition. While the "big names" generally declined to set any of his proposed texts, a surprising number of them, including Schoenberg and Krenek, responded with detailed replies about their creative process. Bahle's "scientific" approach was like a red flag to Hans Pfitzner, who perceived it as yet another effort to murder the mystery of artistic creation (and thereby to stifle creation itself). He responded with yet another book of his own in 1940: *Über musikalische Inspiration* (On musical inspiration), in which he once more defended the extrarational basis of musical creativity. Bahle replied with a new edition of his own book in 1947, in which he was able to dismiss Pfitzner cursorily with a reference to the latter's Nazi leanings.[13]

There is an undeniable irony in Pfitzner's insistence on the "inexpressibility" of inspiration, given his compulsion to express that inexpressibility at great length in various books. There is no less irony in the fact that he was in part raging against men who shared the same (Wagnerian) tradition and whose views on the topic of inspiration were not as dissimilar to his as he (or they) might have wanted to believe. One of the modernists whom Pfitzner despised, Paul Hindemith, found Bahle no more appealing (he described Bahle's book in 1945 as based on the "stammerings of a few pompous, amateur bunglers").[14] The "atonalists" may, as a vague grouping, have been one of Pfitzner's prime targets, but Arnold Schoenberg's views on inspiration were not so different from his own. At roughly the same time that Pfitzner was writing his opera *Palestrina*, in which the creative act is depicted on stage by a Wagner-influenced dream vision, inspiring the protagonist to write his *Missa Papae Marcelli*, Schoenberg was composing a similar metaphor for the *Einfall* in his atonal music drama *Die glückliche Hand*, op. 18 (completed in 1913). There, "The Man" (i.e., the "artist," implicitly Schoenberg) with one hammer blow creates a brilliant diadem and announces to the envious workers thronging around him: "That's how you create jewelry." Not even Pfitzner ever managed such a succinct depiction of the artist of genius to whom the *Einfall* is both the lightning bolt of inspiration and its product, all at once. One of Schoenberg's own greatest fears, a few years after adopting his twelve-tone method, was that the use of a precompositional construct—the note row—might appear to negate the preeminence of "inspiration" in the conception of his music and thus disqualify it from admission to the Austro-German canon. After all, it is difficult to claim spontaneous creativity for basing a work on a "theme" that is not a theme at all, that may comprise only twelve notes, is devoid of rhythmic and harmonic content, and in which no note may be repeated. Schoenberg expended much ink trying to prove that inspiration remained at the core of his music,[15] and the struggle he faced is illuminated not least by the way words sometimes failed him, as we saw in the quotations given at the opening of this chapter. Schoenberg's famous remark to Josef Rufer that his development of the Method had "ensured the hegemony of German music for the next hundred years,"[16] often interpreted as Teutonic arrogance, should rather be seen as an act of overcompensation by a man worried that his discovery might in fact cut him off from that very tradition.

The end of the Second World War and the dying out of Pfitzner's generation saw the end of bitter feuding about inspiration, and while it did not disappear as a topic of interest among either composers or musicologists—Wolfgang Rihm and Karlheinz Stockhausen are just two of the most prominent postwar German composers who have committed their own experiences of inspiration and the compositional process to paper[17]—the *Einfall* no longer occupied the central ground that it had for Pfitzner and others. Adorno severed the *Einfall* from its hitherto synonymous concept of "inspiration" in a long, particularly dense footnote in his *Philosophy of New Music* of 1949: "The 'Einfall' is no psychological category, no matter of 'inspiration,' but a moment in the dialectical process that takes place in the musical form."[18]

In a sense, Adorno marked a shift of the discourse around musical "inspiration" to the English-speaking world, where he had written his *Philosophy* from 1940 to 1948. The first notable study on the topic in English appeared two years before the publication of Adorno's book and was also by a German-speaker in American exile, namely the Viennese critic and psychoanalyst Max Graf: *From Beethoven to Shostakovich: The Psychology of the Composing Process* in 1947. Despite his sometime relationship with Freud and his circle and the book's professed intention to delve into the psychological (its chapter titles include "Childhood Memories," "The Subconscious," and "External and Internal Experiences"), Graf says little that is original when recounting composers' tales of their inspiration, instead offering platitudes aplenty (e.g., "Just as electric waves are intensified in a radio tube, so, too, all experiences are intensified in the soul of a great composer").[19] Arthur Koestler's *The Act of Creation* (London, 1964) focuses more on acts of scientific discovery than on music, but it offers many examples of just what its title says. Koestler draws on a huge array of sources across many centuries, illustrating vividly how tales of "inspiration"—from sudden flashes of insight to creative half-dreams—are remarkably similar, whether told by scientists or by artists, from Archimedes to Descartes, Einstein, or Walter Scott.[20]

The past three decades have seen the publication of two comprehensive studies of musical inspiration in English: Louise Duchesneau's dissertation *The Voice of the Muse: A Study of the Role of Inspiration in Musical Composition* (University of Hamburg 1986) and Jonathan Harvey's *Music and Inspiration* (Faber & Faber, 1999). Duchesneau concentrated on three sources of inspiration: "a metaphysical-religious (the inspiration from ABOVE), a psychological-physiological (the inspiration from INSIDE) and finally a sociological-cultural source (the inspiration from OUTSIDE)."[21] Harvey's work was based on a dissertation (University of Glasgow) that predated Duchesneau's by several years, but in his published book, he took note of her findings. He groups his chapters under not dissimilar headings: "The Composer and the Unconscious," "The Composer and Experience," "The Composer and the Audience" and "The Composer and the Ideal." Harvey had the advantage of being a composer himself, and the most fascinating passages in the book are arguably those about his own experiences of creativity. As he points out, Duchesneau "is at least as concerned with secondary accounts of the process of inspiration, from historians, aestheticians and philosophers, as with composers' own testimonies,"[22] whereas he has chosen to focus on the last of these: "Composers' words, therefore, are at the heart of this book. . . . This is, for better or worse . . . a book by a composer about other composers."[23] Both Duchesneau and Harvey investigate instances of composers being inspired by dreams, nature, religion, life experiences (loves, births, deaths), and by experiencing other works of art. Harvey's composers describe their inspirational experiences in a manner akin to those who responded to Hausegger's questionnaire a hundred years before, though he admits that one must be "sensitive to the possibility that composers deceive . . . there can be no ultimate proof that any composer is telling the truth," referring specifically to the doubts cast by John Deathridge on Wagner's autobiographical accounts of his inspirational moments.[24] This touches on an issue that remains largely unmentioned but lies at the heart of the assorted studies of "inspiration" that we have thus far surveyed: the (often unquestioning) reliance of those who study it on the verbal testimony of those who purport to experience it. Carl Dahlhaus summed up the problem in a lecture on "Wagner's inspiration myths" in 1981 when he observed that "a self-interpretation of the author cannot be the last word on a work, but is merely part of the material of an interpretation—because an author does not speak as such in the moment that he begins to explain himself, but as one exegete among others."[25]

The search for more reliable witnesses of the creative process has been reflected in the increasing importance of sketch studies since the last third of the twentieth century, with more and more composers' manuscripts being subjected to rigorous scrutiny. As in Wagner's day, it is Beethoven studies that have largely paved the way, with groundbreaking work carried out by Kerman, Lockwood, Kinderman, and others. The impact of the Anglo-Saxons on the topic was acknowledged by Hermann Danuser and Günter Katzenberger in their introduction to *Vom Einfall zum Kunstwerk* (From the "Einfall" to the work of art), a series of lectures on twentieth-century music given in Hanover from 1987 to 1989 by leading specialists and published by Laaber in 1993.[26] Danuser in particular documents the efforts of Hausegger, Bahle, and others in investigating the creative act,[27] though this volume as a whole discusses the *Einfall* primarily as just one aspect of the compositional process, with much emphasis on analyses of musical sketches (the authors tend to leave composers' own accounts of their inspiration largely unquestioned).[28]

The present book is more restricted in its scope than Duchesneau's, Harvey's or Danuser's, being a series of case studies in inspiration in

Wagner and four of his Austro-German successors, all of whom had in common a belief in the concept of the *Einfall*. Whatever their shade of opinion on the matter, they all regarded inspiration as something that essentially originates beyond consciousness, be it at times of intense emotion, in the moment between sleeping and waking, or even on the cusp of life and death. More specifically, they supposedly drew their inspiration from musical stimuli (Mahler), the birth of a child (Wagner), a career catastrophe (Furtwängler), the death of a friend or loved one (Mahler, Berg) and even the impending death of the composer himself (Strauss). Furtwängler offers us a case study of a lack of inspiration during a quarter of a century of relative creative silence. Like Harvey, Duchesneau, and before them Bahle, Hausegger, and others, we deal in large part with composers' words, as well as the words of their acolytes and disciples. However, this book aims neither to pinpoint the sources of inspiration, whether "inside," "outside," or "above" the composer, nor to engage directly with the field of sketch studies, though this is probably the most reliable means of investigating the creative process. For our topic here is not the "process"; the aim is rather (in Dahlhaus's terms) to investigate the composer's dual role as author and self-exegete and to see how, and why, the one might inform, confirm, mislead, or contradict the other. Composers' words are thus subjected here to a rigorous investigation, not simply out of a joy in revisionism (though it would be churlish to deny the occasional pleasure of it) but from a desire to reveal the multifaceted nature of an act that composers themselves have often depicted as straightforward. As we shall see, it is often the same men responsible for a musical score of immense complexity who seek after the fact to impose an interpretation on it that is as superficial as the score itself is not. The reasons for such a stance are also investigated (and can in fact add to the layers of meaning of a work). This in turn affords us opportunities to explore the manner in which the supposedly extrarational world of creative inspiration can intersect with the highly rational world of money and politics. We have chosen five composers united by a common language and by similar views on the ways of the muse, not to offer within these clear bounds a concept of inspiration that is smooth and coherent, but rather to lay bare the fissures and inconsistencies within their tradition and their testimonies.

As stated at the outset, the Austro-German tradition to which all our composers belonged took Wagner as its prime representative. Richard Wagner: the self-proclaimed culmination of a self-constructed cultural teleology, at once evangelist, messiah, apostle, and theologian of his own eschatology of art as religion. Who else could have become the *fons et origo* of a mythology of musical inspiration, taking what previous generations had seen as a gift of the Deity and placing it instead wholly within the mind of the composer? His copious writings conjure up a world in which he is at once a product of all those who had gone before and yet somehow apart, springing from the forehead of history like a Valkyrie-Athena, ready-clad in the armor of his ideas. As we shall see, Wagner's notions of inspiration and creativity were themselves anything but new, being derived variously from Schopenhauer and from an extant corpus of commonplaces about the topic. But the immediacy of his descriptions, compounded as they were by the impact of his music, meant that his mythology of the creative act would influence Western musical thought for over a hundred years. So let us begin with him.

CHAPTER ONE

RICHARD WAGNER'S
DYNASTIC DREAMS

R ichard Wagner was not the first German composer to write an autobiography. As a body of scholarly publications on music became established from the mid-eighteenth century onward, composers began to record the facts of their lives for posterity, often prompted by the authors and compilers of the newly emergent encyclopedias and dictionaries. Johann Sebastian Bach might have refused to write anything autobiographical when urged to do so by Johann Mattheson, but others proved more willing. Georg Telemann and Joseph Haydn were among those who provided brief autobiographical sketches for various editors. As the century progressed, composers needed less and less prompting to commit their lives to paper, and the autobiographies of men such as Christian Schubart (1739–91), Carl Ditters von Dittersdorf (1739–99), and others offer firsthand accounts of the musical life of Central Europe. By the time Wagner published his "Autobiographical Sketch" in 1843, it was not unusual for a composer to write about himself, nor was it new to link a man's music with his biography. In his extensive review of Berlioz's *Symphonie fantastique* for the *Neue Zeitschrift für Musik* in 1835, Robert Schumann related that work's program in detail, noting that "the composer wanted to depict several moments from the life of a . . . musician."[1] He tut-tutted the work's obvious tendency to autobiography, finding it distastefully Francophone. The German man, he assured his reader, possessed instead a "shyness before the workplace of genius; he wishes to know nothing of the origins, the tools and secrets of creation . . . let the artist thus shut himself away in his labor pains; we would experience terrible things if we could see all works down to the foundations of their creation."[2]

Wagner was of a different opinion. He knew that the public most definitely wanted to see the artist's "labor pains." His "Autobiographical Sketch" was different from similar texts by his predecessors in that its author was young—not yet out of his twenties—and little known. His *Rienzi* had only just been premiered in October 1842, and his *Flying Dutchman* on January 2, 1843, both in Dresden; and in the wake of his success he was appointed kapellmeister there in early February. Wagner was thus an up-and-coming talent, and his *Dutchman* was due for a performance in Berlin in March. The magazine *Zeitung für die elegante Welt*, edited by an old family friend, Heinrich Laube, afforded Wagner the chance of some publicity in advance of his Berlin premiere with a two-part autobiography published on February 1 and February 8, 1843. Wagner seized the opportunity to offer his readers certain insights into just those "origins, tools, and secrets of creation" that Schumann had felt so sure they did not want. It was the shape of things to come.

Wagner accordingly offered a brief introduction to his life and works hitherto, smoothing over its many rough edges and praising Meyerbeer as much as he would later pillory him. Of particular interest to us here is his tale of his stormy sea voyage from Riga to London and how it inspired his *Flying Dutchman*. Eight years later, when in exile in Zurich after his participation in the failed Dresden uprising of 1849, Wagner wrote a far longer, far more detailed autobiographical text: his *Communication to My Friends*, a book of reminiscences published with the libretti to his *Dutchman*, *Tannhäuser*, and *Lohengrin*. The story of the stormy sea voyage and its impact on the *Dutchman* is here elaborated once more. But as John Deathridge has observed, the link between the stormy sea voyage and the opera was a fabrication, a tale invented in order to help promote the work.[3] Wagner does not stop at that in his *Communication*, for he also couples sketching the libretto for *Tannhäuser* with having seen the Wartburg for the first time (another falsehood, but one he would expand upon at greater length in his later autobiography *Mein Leben*).

Wagner's *Communication to My Friends* proved vital in bringing Wagner together with his future patrons Otto and Mathilde Wesendonck; Mathilde was supposedly quite taken by it. Whether or not this convinced Wagner of the efficaciousness of detailing his creative "labor pains" in autobiographical form, he now showed an increasing keenness to record such details in both his letters and his writings. Since settling in Zurich, he had established himself as the prime musical mover in the city, conducting its orchestra and reorganizing its concert life. His endeavors culminated in a massive festival of his works in May 1853. But since completing *Lohengrin* in 1848, he had composed almost nothing, having spent his time instead developing theories for a music drama "of the future" and writing the libretti for four operas based on old Germanic myths, his *Ring des Nibelungen*. In November 1853 he finally embarked on the composition of the first evening of his tetralogy, *Das Rheingold*, and his work proceeded with unprecedented rapidity. A year later, in a letter of December 29, 1854, to his patron Emilie Ritter of Dresden, he described the moment in Italy in autumn 1853 when his inspiration had flowed at last. This "vision of La Spezia" would later become his most famous tale of inspiration:

> Already in Spezzia [*sic*] I had a complete vision: in a state of terrible suffering of the nerves, with a sense of revulsion toward everything that my eye saw, I lay down a little one day in order to defend myself with closed eyes against the most hideous discomposure: when for a moment I had sunk into a certain half-sleep, suddenly the instrumental introduction to the Rheingold appeared before me with such clarity and certainty, something which I had never been able to determine properly; thus I suddenly understood what was up with me. In that moment I decided to return, and to give up the whole outside world. An hour afterwards I sat in the carriage to return, and with crazy haste I hurried back over the Alps . . . finally, back home, I began my work: it flew from my pen [literally: "from my hand"]![4]

As commentators have observed, it is odd that Wagner—never one to keep a good tale to himself—should have waited a year to tell someone about this. The fact that his letter insists on the immediacy of his experience so many times suggests that he is compensating for this delay. The "vision" is indeed mentioned in Wagner's "Annals" for 1853: "Dysentery. Steam ship to Spezzia: ill. Bad lodgings. Sick. Try second day: walk; hill of pine forests. Afternoon sleep on the couch: wake up with conception of the instrumental introduction to the *Rheingold* (E-flat major triad): sinking in the babbling waters. Immediate decision to return and commence work."[5] But as has also been observed, it is likely that this entry was made retrospectively, in the 1860s, not long before Wagner dictated the following, more elaborate version to Cosima for his autobiography *Mein Leben* in 1868:

> My dysentery grew on account of seasickness and, in the most exhausted state, barely able to drag myself onward, I sought and found in Spezia the best guest house, which to my horror lay in a narrow, noisy street. After a night spent in feverishness and sleeplessness, I compelled myself the

next day to embark on a long hike through the hilly environment, which was covered in pine forests. Everything seemed bare and barren and I did not understand what I was doing here. Returning home in the afternoon, I stretched out, dead tired, on a hard daybed in order to await the long-yearned-for hour of sleep. It did not come; instead I sank into a kind of somnambulant state in which I suddenly received a sensation as if I was sinking in strongly flowing water. The rushing of the waters soon took on musical form as an E-flat-major chord that surged on unceasingly as a figured arpeggiation. These arpeggios appeared as increasingly animated melodic figurations, but the pure triad of E-flat major never changed, its persistence seeming to give an unending significance to the element into which I sank. With a feeling as if the waves were now roaring away and above me, I awoke in abrupt terror from my half-sleep. I immediately recognized that the orchestral introduction to the *Rheingold* that I had carried around in me but which I had not been able to pinpoint had appeared to me: and I quickly understood what the root of it was for me: the stream of life was to flow to me not from without, but from within.[6]

John Deathridge was the first to observe that this story must be a fabrication, as it does not match the known chronology of the composition of the *Rheingold*'s prelude. Nor is this the last such inspirational story to be found in Wagner's writings, which makes the disentanglement of fact and fiction in them such an immensely complex task. On one occasion he did at least admit to his embellishment of the truth, namely in his account in *Mein Leben* of having conceived the three acts of *Parsifal* in his new home in Zurich, the "Asyl," on Good Friday morning in 1857.[7] The sheer facts make this an impossibility (Wagner only moved into the "Asyl" after Good Friday), and two decades later he confessed to his second wife Cosima that he had made it up—though if it hadn't been a Good Friday, he said, it had certainly felt like one.

Carl Dahlhaus observed that Wagner's "nature" inspirations—the stormy sea for the *Holländer* and the visions of La Spezia and Good Friday—had most probably been influenced by Goethe's account in the second part of his *Italian Journey* of how a beautiful garden in Palermo and the ancient theater of Taormina had inspired him to sketch out his *Nausikka* drama.[8] John Deathridge has pointed to a more contemporary source for the "La Spezia" vision, for Wagner's letter to Julie Ritter dates from shortly after he was introduced to the writings of Schopenhauer by his friend Georg Herwegh in the autumn of 1854. Wagner's account is clearly indebted to the philosopher's essay "Versuch über das Geistersehen" (On seeing spirits) in his volume *Parerga und Paralipomena*. There, Schopenhauer discusses the psychological import of "half-sleep" and similar trancelike states[9] and also describes specifically how an "acute fever" can produce hallucinations that include sound, as well as other sensations.[10]

It is noteworthy that both the La Spezia and the Good Friday inspirations were committed to paper for patrons to read (his autobiography had been begun specifically to inform King Ludwig of Bavaria about his life hitherto), as these instances of quasi-divine inspiration were presumably intended to impress upon his patrons the worthiness of the cause to which their coffers were devoted. While it was neither Wagner's first nor last autobiographical tweak, the "La Spezia" vision remains particularly significant because it links Wagner's genius with his subconscious and offers the first concrete proof of the impact that Schopenhauer's thought was having on him. What had primarily attracted Wagner to the philosopher was the unique significance accorded to music in his principal work *Die Welt als Wille und Vorstellung* (The world as will and representation). Referring to the "Will" – for him the primeval driving force behind the world—Schopenhauer writes that "music is namely just such an *unmediated* objectification of the Will, and a mirror of it, as the world is itself . . . that is why the impact of music is so much more powerful and insistent than that of the other arts: for these only speak of a shadow, while music speaks of the being itself."[11]

It was not until his essay "Beethoven" of 1870, however, that Wagner discussed Schopenhauer's impact upon him in detail in a text written for the general public. This essay is ostensibly in celebration of the hundredth birthday of Ludwig van, as its simple, stark title suggests (though "Beethoven" was not Wagner's first choice; that had been "Beethoven und die deutsche Nation," Beethoven and the German nation). Its impact on the reception history of Beethoven was immense. His late works had hitherto been largely misunderstood by both public and critical opinion alike, but Wagner's insistence upon their significance now helped to turn the tables. Over the next few decades, Wagner's positive opinion of them became the norm. It is possible, too, that Wagner felt a need to wrest Beethoven back from the attention accorded him by the newly emergent field of musicology in Germany. In the early 1860s Gustav Nottebohm was made responsible for a new, complete edition of Beethoven's works. His close analysis of the sketches culminated in 1865 in the first-ever publication of a transcription of one of Beethoven's sketchbooks (entitled simply *Ein Skizzenbuch von Beethoven*). Nottebohm was not the only Beethoven scholar to emerge in the 1860s. Alexander Thayer published the first volume of his Beethoven biography (in German) in 1866,[12] and Ludwig Nohl and Ludwig von Köchel independently began publishing letters of Beethoven in 1865.[13] In 1864 Otto Jahn had published an article entitled "Beethoven und die Ausgaben seiner Werke" (Beethoven and the editions of his works) in which he similarly insisted on "scrupulousness" and "philological criticism" as the essential basis of a modern, scholarly edition.[14] Like Nottebohm, he emphasized the importance of consulting the composer's sketchbooks.[15] Jahn specifically mentions Beethoven's own "complaints" about those who offered fanciful interpretations of his works and their inspiration, and remarks:

> It is possible that a succinct, sensual impression at an opportune moment might in a flash [*blitzartig*] call forth a characteristic motive; it is possible too that the impression of this would remain fixed in the artist's memory; but this external stimulation has nothing more to do with the artistic development of this germ, with the creative organization of the work of art. The activity of the artist moves in quite different regions and whoever believes that a work of art can be constructed through random external events has no idea of artistic creation.[16]

But where Nottebohm, Jahn, and others believed they could analyze and comprehend Beethoven's works by examining the extant sources to ascertain his working methods, Wagner took a contrary path, emphasizing the composer's "genius" and intuition and focusing on precisely those external stimuli derided by Jahn. Wagner mentions no one by name, but opens his essay on the composer with a disparaging swipe at those who wanted to use the methods of "foolish" literary historians to explain Beethoven's development. Beethoven's works are in themselves, according to Wagner, "incomprehensible,"[17] the composer "a complete secret,"[18] and to "wish to explain [his] works themselves would be a foolish undertaking."[19] "Of him is true what Schopenhauer says of the musician in general: he speaks the greatest wisdom in a language that no reason can understand."[20] We know from Wagner's letters and Cosima's diaries that he was aware of the work of Jahn and Nottebohm,[21] and we can safely assume that he was unsympathetic to both, for Nottebohm was a former student of Mendelssohn and Schumann and a friend of Brahms, while Jahn had long made public his antipathy to Wagner's music (he had once even declared that Wagner's *Tannhäuser* displayed his dependence on "Meyerbeerism").[22] Furthermore, Wagner might have feared that if Beethoven could be thus dissected by these new musical philologists, then he might himself at some future date be subjected to similar analytical attention. Far better to second-guess them all by trying to determine the reception of his work in advance. It is thus a matter of some irony that it was probably the field of sketch studies, which in our own day has played a major role in revealing and detailing the creative process, that prompted Wagner to stake a claim for the composer as only true exegete of his works (and as we shall see in the next chapter, at least one of Wagner's successors went one step further by actually destroying his own sketches so as to prevent latter-day Nottebohms from dissecting them).

The unambiguousness of the title "Beethoven" and the influence exerted by the book help to disguise the fact that it is as much about Wagner as about Beethoven. In fact, after mentioning Beethoven at the beginning, Wagner then proceeds to ignore him for fourteen pages. His name is not even mentioned in more than twenty percent of the whole book. Given Wagner's teleological view of music history, this makes a certain sense; for if one regards one's own work as the culmination of one's predecessors', then whatever one writes about them refers implicitly, if not explicitly, to oneself. Wagner had long insisted that his music drama was the full realization of what Beethoven had intimated in the last movement of his Ninth Symphony. In closer proximity to "Beethoven," we find in Wagner's 1868 tract *On Conducting* a discussion of the "thematic web" in the latter's symphonies, though it is obvious that Wagner was really talking about the "thematic web" to be found in his own *Ring of the Nibelung* (he had only recently recommended work on it after a long hiatus). Beethoven's immense popularity and acknowledged historical significance in nineteenth-century Germany made of him a useful tool for Wagner to affirm his own position in history.

Wagner's "Beethoven" thus exists in a fluid continuum with Wagner's "Wagner," the one merging into the other. In "Beethoven," they both merge with Wagner's "Schopenhauer" when Wagner uses the philosopher to help explain the origins of creativity in a long preamble to his actual discussion of Beethoven. He writes that "musical conception . . . can originate only in the aspect of consciousness which Schopenhauer defines as introverted"; this "introverted consciousness" in turn can only be perceived by means of what Wagner, following Schopenhauer, calls the body's "dream organ." The "world of sound," says Wagner, is to the "world of light" what the dream is to the waking state. Musical creativity is thus, he says, akin to a state of clairvoyance, which affords the composer a state of "rapture" unlike any other to be had in the arts. Wagner even reinvents Beethoven's deafness as a source of the composer's creative strength, forcing him to turn his aural "gaze" inward as kind of latter-day Tiresias[23]—or even "a saint."[24] Near-sainthood can be attained by others too:

> Only one condition can surpass [that of the musician]: that of the saint,
> because this condition is continuous and unsullied, whereas the raptur-
> ous clairvoyance of the musician has to alternate constantly with the re-
> turn of a state of individual consciousness that must be regarded as all
> the more mournful since the excited state had raised him higher than all
> confines of individuality. It is this last reason, his suffering, with which he
> must pay for his state of ecstasy, the state in which he delights us so unut-
> terably. In this the musician may appear to us again as more worthy of
> veneration than other artists, indeed he might even seem almost to pos-
> sess a claim to sainthood. For in truth, the relation of his art to the whole
> gamut of all the other arts is like that of *religion* to the *church*.[25]

Wagner retains Schopenhauer's notion, expressed in the *Versuch*, that the
dreams we experience during our deepest sleep are remembered in "allegorical" dreams that occur before we awake: it is only *these* dreams that we
are then able to recall. He now uses this as a metaphor for music's relationship to the other arts. Just as the dream of deepest sleep needs the allegorical dream to reach general consciousness, he says, so do the other arts need
sound (i.e., music) in order to gain access to the exterior world. "[Music]
calls; and in the counter-call it recognizes itself again: thus call and counter-call become a consoling game it plays with itself, climaxing in a playful state of rapture."[26] Wagner now recounts two instances from his own
biography (not Beethoven's, who has for the moment been forgotten) in
order to illustrate "the dreamlike state into which a sympathetic ear places
[one]."[27] The first is an account of a sleepless night that he spent in Venice
when he heard gondoliers calling to each other along the canals. The second is a daytime example: once, when walking in the Alps in Canton Uri,
he heard cowherds yodeling to each other across the wide valleys. He proceeds to illustrate these anecdotes in turn with another metaphor: "Thus
the child awakes after a night in the mother's lap with a cry of desire, and is
answered by the soothing caresses of its mother."[28] Wagner continues this
argument by stating that the experience of a "truly moving work of music"
can place concert-goers in "a state that has a fundamental similarity to that
of somnambulist clairvoyance."

   Thus to sum up: to Wagner (writing with the implicit authority of
Schopenhauer), music is a bridge between the inner and outer forms of
consciousness, a link to the clairvoyant dream-state both for the composer
and for his listeners. It is, in a sense, also a quasi-religion. The musician
(most particularly the composer) is the man able to channel its rapture
and thus attain quasi-holy status (this essay thus also clearly foreshad-
ows Wagner's later, so-called regeneration writings, in which art is openly

assigned the status of an ersatz religion). The source of music is located in the composer's own innermost consciousness—hence, no doubt, that mention in his account of La Spezia that "the stream of life was to flow to me not from without, but from within." And when Wagner offers a concrete analogy between the phenomenon of the dream and the conception of a musical work, he turns to Beethoven's C-sharp-minor quartet, stating that its opening is "like waking on the morning of a day" in which "the innermost dream image becomes awakened in the loveliest remembrance."[29] This moment between sleeping and waking was of central importance to Wagner, as we also saw in his account of the "vision" of La Spezia, committed to paper less than two years before his "Beethoven" essay.

This dense, prolix, repetitive, unfocused essay with its many *non sequiturs* and its metaphors of metaphors demonstrates a degree of sophistry that is breathtaking, even for Wagner. Autobiographical anecdotes alternate with ornate semianalysis of Beethoven's late works; and when Wagner stresses how Beethoven's deafness turned him into a "seer" and a "saint," the implication is that Wagner is a man who has attained these same levels of consciousness without the compulsion of physical disability. Nor can Wagner resist a final flourish, linking all his notions of creativity and consciousness with the victories of Germany in the ongoing war against France—a kind of *non* to end all *sequiturs*.

Wagner accords his essay a veneer of scholarly rectitude by including footnotes and page numbers for his references to Schopenhauer's *Welt als Wille und Vorstellung* (this was unusual for him, and is perhaps added proof that he saw himself in competition for Beethoven's legacy with the upcoming scholarly caste). He also adopts Schopenhauer's highfalutin language ("*Traumorgan*," "*fatidike Träume*," "*allegorische Träume*," and the like). But for all this, it still seems at times as if Wagner had made a selection of his favorites among the man's cornucopia of ideas, placed them in a hat, then drawn them out one by one in random order as in a Dadaist poem *avant la lettre*. His understanding of Schopenhauer was perhaps not much greater than Schopenhauer's knowledge of music (which was limited, to judge from his discussion of it in *Die Welt als Wille und Vorstellung*). Wagner tended to pick and choose only what appealed to him—thus, for example, he studiously ignored Schopenhauer's aversion to the erotic and his overall ascetic imperatives, for they were incompatible with his own compulsive desire for silks, scents, and sex. He had discovered Schopenhauer's "philosophy of renunciation" at the moment when he was coming to terms with the need to renounce any notion of sexual union with Mathilde Wesendonck. This synchronicity, and the supreme position that Schopenhauer afforded to music, were no doubt the two things about him that Wagner found most compelling at the time. (Although Wagner later announced to Mathilde his realization that the true fulfillment of Schopenhauer actually lay in "sexual love," she still refused to sleep with him). Wagner's alighting upon the *Versuch*, with its involved discussion of dreams, also seems to have coincided with his own growing interest in dreams. To be sure, the greater number of dream discussions to be found in his letters and writings from the 1850s onward also coincides with an increase in the sheer number of extant written sources available, so we cannot make any objectively reliable claims about Wagner's apparently increasing fascination with the topic. But we do know it was an interest that he shared with Mathilde Wesendonck, for their correspondence confirms it, and it was not by chance that one of her poems that he set was entitled "Träume" (Dreams).

Wagner and Schopenhauer were not the first men to be fascinated by the creative aspect of dreams, somnambulism and trancelike states; as mentioned in the introduction, Arthur Koestler's *The Act of Creation* lists a whole host of artists and scientists before and after them who found the boundary between sleeping and waking a stimulant to creative thought.[30] Dreams and semiconscious states have also been depicted in literature and drama for as long as these arts have existed (witness Homer and Aeschylus). The history of opera, too, is littered with scenes of dreams, half-waking visions and sleepwalkers, all of which were two-a-penny in the repertoire that Wagner had conducted as a hack kapellmeister in the little theaters of Germany back in the 1830s. From the late eighteenth century onward—the moment when science ceased being the exclusive province of intellectuals and began to impinge visibly on the lives of the middle classes—a veritable fad had developed around the topic of dreams, trances, and the so-called animal magnetism allied to them, as postulated by Franz Anton Mesmer in his quack healing practices (also mentioned glowingly in Schopenhauer's *Versuch*, but ignored by Wagner when he drew upon the tract). We know that Wagner possessed at least one other book on dreams in his library, namely Gotthilf Heinrich von Schubert's *Die Symbolik des Traumes*,[31] though it was a book of which Schopenhauer himself took a dim view ("of no use except for its title," he wrote of it in his *Versuch*).[32] By this time, the opium-induced dream had stimulated the artistic imagination even further, as in Coleridge's "Kubla Khan," subtitled "a vision in a dream" and whose purported origins in the poppy seed are explained openly in its author's preface. Closer to our topic is the program of Berlioz's *Symphonie fantastique*, with its opium-sodden hero. But Wagner was the first composer who tried to construct a psychological, theoretical framework (however pseudo in its science) linking music in general, and musical creativity in particular, with dreamlike states of consciousness. The significance that he accords dream states in "Beethoven" also helps to explain why he found it necessary for Cosima to record his own dreams with such meticulous precision in her diaries.

It was not just in his writings and in his wife's diaries that Wagner engaged with dream states. As befitted a composer versant in the German, French, and Italian traditions (and one who knew his Shakespeare, too), he assigned crucial dramatic roles to dreams and visions in several of his own works, ranging from Senta's vision of the *Dutchman* to Tristan's delirium and Hagen's quasi-hypnotic trance in his scene with Alberich in *Götterdämmerung*. The extant literature on these scenes is vast; in the present instance, however, we shall focus on a possible cross-fertilization between "Beethoven" and the nonvocal work that Wagner composed immediately after it: the *Siegfried Idyll*.

The *Idyll* is one of just two mature works by Wagner for small ensemble, the other being "Träume" (Dreams) in its version for violin solo and small orchestra. It is important to consider the circumstances of performance of this earlier work, for they largely determined those of the *Idyll*. This was one of a set of five songs to texts by his adored Mathilde Wesendonck that Wagner began in autumn 1857 at about the same time that he embarked upon *Tristan und Isolde*. Three were completed before the end of the year ("Der Engel" in late November 1857; "Träume" in early December; and "Schmerzen" in mid-December). Of these, Wagner chose to orchestrate "Träume" for solo violin and small orchestra to be performed as a birthday gift for Mathilde on December 23 (at a time, conveniently, when her husband had not yet returned from an urgent business trip to America). The forces involved (besides the soloist) were four violins, two violas, one cello, two clarinets, two bassoons, and two horns. Wagner assembled his musicians early in the morning and also procured a local wind band to perform enough other pieces to make a decent program. They played at the bottom of the stairs in the foyer, one floor below Mathilde's bedroom. Wagner's wife Minna—who at this time was still on speaking terms with Mathilde—was roped in to help make refreshments. The event was talked about widely enough for Cosima von Bülow to hear of it. She did not yet know Wagner well, but she knew enough to remark facetiously in a letter to her friend Emma Herwegh how Wagner had written "a serenade for his pretty Mathilde."[33]

Thirteen years after Mathilde's birthday music, Wagner wrote another serenade, this time for Cosima herself. She had by now borne him three children; they had married in mid-1870, after her divorce from Hans von Bülow. Cosima's birthday fell one day after that of Mathilde, but she always celebrated it one day later still, on Christmas Day itself (and from here on, whenever Cosima's "birthday" is mentioned, we shall mean the twenty-fifth). This birthday serenade was what we know as the *Siegfried Idyll*. Hans Richter, Wagner's odd-job-man-about-the-house, was tasked with organizing the ensemble for the occasion, as he recalled thirty-nine years later in a letter to Theodor Müller-Reuter.[34] The musicians were chosen from the members of the Zurich Tonhalle Orchestra—the successor to the Zurich orchestra that Wagner had himself conducted in the early 1850s. There was one rehearsal in the foyer of the Zurich City Theater on December 21 (directed by Richter) then another (under Wagner's baton) on the afternoon of the twenty-fourth in the hall of the Hôtel du Lac in Lucerne. The musicians stayed overnight in Lucerne and arrived at the Tribschen villa at 7:30 a.m. on Cosima's birthday to perform the *Idyll* on the staircase outside her salon. The orchestra comprised four violins, two violas (the second—Hans Richter—doubling trumpet), one cello, double bass, two horns, one trumpet (doubling viola—Richter again), two clarinets and one each of flute, oboe, and bassoon. Richter's letter to Müller-Reuter included a description of how the musicians were arranged on the stairs, and a little sketch to make matters clear. Wagner had been unable to see the cello and double bass, so Richter stood where he could see both them and the conductor and relayed the latter's gestures during the performance. Later that same day, Wagner gave several repeat performances of the work in the salon on the ground floor. Cosima recorded the incident in her diary as follows:

> As I awoke, my ears perceived a sound that swelled up more and more until I could no longer believe I was dreaming. Music was sounding, and what music! When it had died away, Richard came to me with the five children and presented me with the score of the "Symphonic Birthday Greeting." I was in tears, but so was the whole house. Richard had placed his orchestra on the stairs and in this manner consecrated our Tribschen forever! It's the "Tribschen Idyll," that's the name of the work.... After breakfast, the orchestra set itself up again, the Idyll was played again in the lower rooms, and moved us all.... "Let me die now," I cried to Richard.[35]

If one listens from Cosima's former bedroom to the work as it is played behind closed doors on the staircase—as she did, at least at the start—then it becomes clear that the opening of the work, with its two "false starts" before the "real" one (on B, E and G♯ respectively), must have been intended as a kind of ritualistic, threefold waking-call, each more insistent (higher in tessitura and more dissonant) than the one before it ("swelling up more and more" in Cosima's words; see ex. 1.1).[36] It is as if Wagner had written it in order to pause briefly each time and listen to whether Cosima was already stirring. It also corresponds with uncanny accuracy to the description in "Beethoven," quoted above, of how music enters consciousness: "Thus call and counter-call become a consoling game it plays with itself, climaxing in a playful state of rapture"—though here, it is the same ensemble providing call and counter-call, not two gondoliers or cowherds a canal or an alp apart.

The strings are at the beginning barely perceptible from the bedroom, which throws the first entry of the woodwind into particular relief. If Cosima was indeed waking up only as the work began, then this woodwind entry would have been the first thing of which she became properly aware. Appropriately, it is the flute playing the so-called slumber motive taken from the close of the *Walküre* (and at the same pitch as there; see ex. 1.2). If it seems odd that Wagner intended to wake Cosima with the music that sent Brünnhilde to sleep, we must remember that this motive also sounds in the third act of *Siegfried* before Brünnhilde is awakened. Since Wagner seemed keen for Cosima to see herself as the inspiration for his Brünnhilde (at least in her incarnation in *Siegfried* and *Götterdämmerung*), then the significance of using Brünnhilde's waking music to wake Cosima will have been obvious to her. She will have found further confirmation in the fact that the work's main theme is the same one we find in the third act of *Siegfried* after the title hero has woken Brünnhilde (the passage "Ewig war ich," whose music Wagner had ostensibly conceived in 1864 when he and Cosima consummated their relationship in a cottage by the Starnberg lake).[37]

Let us consider again Cosima's diary entry for her birthday: "As I awoke, my ears perceived a sound that swelled up more and more until I could no longer believe I was dreaming. Music was sounding, and what music!" she wrote. Wagner thus planned his *Idyll* to begin while Cosima was in that transition period between deep sleep and the act of waking up, the period (according to both him and Schopenhauer) when allegorical dreams regurgitate the content of the dreams of deep sleep in order to bring them into full consciousness. To quote his own comment on Beethoven's C-sharp-minor Quartet, the opening of the *Idyll* was presumably intended to be "like waking on the morning of a day"

Example 1.1. Wagner, opening of the *Siegfried Idyll*, mm. 1–21, with the three "waking calls."

in which "the innermost dream image becomes awakened in the loveliest remembrance."

"Träume" had been similarly conceived in its ensemble version as an *aubade* for its dedicatee, though decorum meant that it was performed one floor below her, and the bustle of musicians and servants will have ensured that she was awake and decently dressed in order to appear before the assembled throng (Mathilde was almost certainly warned in advance so that she would not emerge in a state of indecency from her boudoir before so many members of the lower classes). But the familiar setting of the *Idyll* and the fact that he was serenading his spouse, not a married muse, allowed Wagner to go one step further and enact a "staging" of the moment of inspiration, though one in which the person "inspired" to music is not him but his wife, while the music to which she is inspired in her state of half-sleep is not hers, but his. Since Cosima knew the "Beethoven" essay inside out, she would have understood it thus as well.

This is in one sense a demonstration of control: even when she is in a state of sleep, the music tells us, Cosima's thoughts may only be of Wagner and his music, and when she is "inspired" in that state, she still has no independent consciousness. Wagner had written in "Beethoven" that stimuli of the "Will" had to be absent in the moment of creating or appreciating art, but it was perhaps easier for him (maybe even tempting) to imagine expunging Cosima's will rather than his own. It was not the first time that Wagner had acted as if she had no independent existence. Cosima's diary entry for the day of Siegfried's birth, for example, is written in the first person, but is in Wagner's hand (in other words, it is written by Wagner in the first person, as if he were Cosima). Anyone reading Cosima's diaries cannot but notice how she repeatedly subjugates herself (though this might also have been a stratagem to gain a covert dominance over her husband).

Cosima's birthday in 1870 was not the last time that Wagner performed the *Idyll* for her as she was waking up, which suggests that the staging of the work was to him an integral part of it. If its purpose was to impose on Cosima what Wagner wanted her to think, it might also have been to obscure something else that he *didn't* want her to think, that he wanted to conceal from her, or that he wanted to cancel out, and perhaps those repeat performances on the border of sleep and waking all had a similar intention. While this by necessity remains supposition, one matter that Wagner might have wished unthought-of could have been the birth, just

Example 1.2. Wagner, *Siegfried Idyll*, mm. 35–39.

eight months before Siegfried's, of a son, Wilhelm, to their maid Vreneli. It has long been suspected that Wagner was the father (this scandal has recently surfaced again in the press, as Vreneli's grandson is at the moment of writing still alive and bears a striking facial resemblance to the Wagner family).[38] But there was one event of which Cosima knew full well and that we know Wagner would have dearly liked her to forget: the birthday serenade he had written for Mathilde Wesendonck thirteen years before. While it might seem to us that composing a serenade for Cosima would merely serve to remind her of its predecessor, it seems likely that Wagner himself believed a bigger, better serenade for his wife would be the best way to exorcise or expunge the memory of his former muse.

The *Idyll* is indeed a far more substantial work than "Träume," a statement on Wagner's part that its dedicatee was of greater importance to him than had been her predecessor. Yet we could not blame Cosima if on that Christmas Day in the morning she pondered whether Wagner might be becoming a serial perpetrator in birthday serenading, nor if in some recess of her mind she worried about whether she might not yet be the last woman to be thus serenaded. She had produced Wagner an heir, so she may have felt reassured as to the security of her position, but this would not have halted her unease at having been preceded by another. For of all the women in Wagner's life, it was only Mathilde Wesendonck who succeeded in instilling in Cosima a deep, undying sense of unease and dislike, and Wagner was aware enough of the intensity of her jealousy always to play down Mathilde's significance in his biography and his music (nor did time soften Cosima's grudges, for long after Wagner's death she did her utmost to ensure—not wholly successfully—that Mathilde's correspondence with Richard was destroyed).[39] The theatricality of the *Idyll*'s first performance was surely intended to offer further assurance to Cosima of her unassailable status by trying to expunge the ghosts of "Träume." Goodness knows what Cosima would have thought, had she found out that Mathilde had heard her *Idyll* first. For as Hans Richter's above-mentioned letter confirms, Mathilde and Otto had been present at the first rehearsal in the foyer of the old Zurich City Theater on December 21, 1870. Given Wagner's debt to them and the fact that they were patrons of the Tonhalle Orchestra whose musicians were performing the *Idyll*, Wagner probably had no choice but to let them in (it is not impossible that they even paid the fees of the musicians).

The *Idyll*, then, was perhaps less a demonstration of control on Wagner's part than a considered delegation of it to Cosima. By staging the work as Cosima's "dream inspiration" after the manner described in his "Beethoven" essay, Wagner was sharing the work entire with her (or at least purporting to). He was assigning her proprietary rights to it, a degree of equivalency in its conception and authorship—in a manner that he still determined, to be sure, but which would have been significant nonetheless to Cosima herself. If it was meant as a kind of forfeit or pledge to reassure her of her uniqueness in his life, she certainly treated the work henceforth as her personal, private possession. She was pained whenever outsiders heard it and was mortified when Wagner finally sold it to his publisher in 1877 in order to cover financial debts.[40] One must wonder if she ever quite forgave him for it. She would have known that Wagner had hesitated before selling the *Wesendonck Lieder* to Schott fifteen years before, another time when money matters had proved pressing. Cosima had in the meantime become so convinced that the *Idyll* was "her" work, that for it to suffer the same fate as Mathilde's birthday serenade must have made her feel that she was not quite as unique as Wagner had let her believe. To add insult to injury, the sale happened at just the time when Cosima had become particularly aware of Wagner's passion for Judith Gautier. Maybe she feared that he might be planning his next birthday serenade already. At least, she must have realized that the *Idyll* had never really belonged to her at all.

There is one final possible correlation between the *Siegfried Idyll* and "Beethoven" that can shed light on the actual source of the work's inspiration, situating it far from anything subconscious. Where "Beethoven" was intended to cement Wagner's own place in music history—implicitly as Beethoven's one true heir—the *Siegfried Idyll* celebrates the birth of Wagner's own heir, the boy whose name figures in its title. The subsequent domestic performances of the *Idyll* in the Wagner family home were regularly coupled with Richard recounting the tale of Siegfried's birth, which confirms the significance of the boy in the work's quasi-programmatic content. On July 7, 1878, Cosima even commented in her diary that "R. sings from the Idyll 'A son is born!'" though we sadly do not know which passage it was, nor whether it had been conceived to accompany these specific words.[41] But Wagner had more than his own prospective dynasty in mind, as the close of "Beethoven" also makes evident. After the Prussian victory against France at the time of the *Idyll*'s conception in late 1870, it was clear to many that King Wilhelm of Prussia would soon be crowned Emperor of a united Germany (Wagner and Cosima had already discussed the possibility of this several months before, in August 1870).[42] Wagner had realized that the rising tide of German nationalism might help him in his grand project of finding a home for his operatic cycle on Germanic myths. As early as December 12, 1870, Cosima noted: "[Richard] says I should write to Countess Bismarck that the German Kaiser is predestined; he needs a Kaiser for his artwork of the future."[43] Just five days after the first performance of the *Idyll*, three weeks before Wilhelm was actually proclaimed Emperor in Versailles, Wagner received an offer of 1500 francs from the publishing house of C. F. Peters for a coronation march for the emperor-to-be (the very man, let us not forget, whose armies had crushed those of Wagner's patron King Ludwig five years before). Cosima noted that same day that Richard absolutely couldn't write on demand, and certainly not a coronation march—but the score of the *Kaisermarsch* was nevertheless finished within ten weeks and appeared in print four weeks after that. The March closes with a ghastly chorus to a patriotic hymn text that Wagner penned himself. It was too late to be a coronation march, but was at least performed on May 5, 1871, in Berlin in the presence of the new Kaiser.

The proximity of the *Idyll* to the *Kaisermarsch* has hitherto received little attention, for the difference in quality between them is vast. But if the former is performed at the brisk tempo that seems to have been Wagner's own preference,[44] then its climactic passages at times sound almost triumphalist, with more than a hint of the *Kaisermarsch* about them. Their thematic material is also related, with their chains of interlocking, descending fourths in each case strikingly similar to the theme from the last act of *Siegfried* that German commentators call the "Love union motive." Wagner's increasing concern with posterity was reflected in 1870/71 in the publication of the first volume of his autobiography and in his plan for a complete edition of all his writings. The birth of a son had now turned this concern into a consideration of matters positively dynastic. The *Siegfried Idyll* and the *Kaisermarsch* both celebrate the birth of a new dynasty, with Wagner well aware that the fate of his own might be assured by the favor of the other. If in "Beethoven" Wagner paints himself as a metaphorical "son-of-Beethoven," then it seems he already had dreams of Siegfried following in his footsteps as a kind of "son-of-son-of-Beethoven," for on January 4, 1871, Cosima wrote that "R. calls Fidi a blond Beethoven. He thinks he looks like him."[45] Perhaps the most conclusive proof of his dynastic concerns lies in the parody that Wagner made of his *Kaisermarsch* for Cosima's next birthday "serenade." Exactly one year after the first performance of the *Idyll*, Wagner had his children sing the tune of the *Kaisermarsch* for Cosima using new words: "Heil! Heil der Mutter!" (Hail! Hail to the mother!) and "Heil Deinem Siegfried! Unserem Fidi" (Hail to your Siegfried! To our Fidi!).[46] As Adorno once remarked, "One usually parodies that to which . . . one is drawn."[47] So Wagner's replacing the Kaiser in his *Kaisermarsch* with his own wife and son tells us much about his broader intentions and aspirations.

There is no contradiction in claiming that the *Siegfried Idyll* was prompted by Wagner's dynastic delight and the rosy prospects of a future linked to the fate of his ascendant nation, and at the same time was a vehicle for expressing in music his own quasi-Schopenhauerian notions about the origins of the creative act. Indeed, the *Idyll* offers us a prime example of how utopian fantasy and hard-nosed calculation, the private and the public, and inspiration and perspiration can all come together in a work of art.

With his visions of La Spezia, the visions in his "Beethoven," and his insistence on the boundary between waking and sleeping as key to artistic inspiration, Wagner set an example that would be followed by innumerable composers after him. Soon it would seem as if *every* serious German composer had to have a vision. Crucially, in assigning the composer a priestlike status in his quasi-religion of art, capable of accessing divine truths through the portal of the unconscious, Wagner set up his readers to accept his dicta on creativity without question. His subjective web of half-truths and insinuations may have been intended solely to cement his position in history, but it was assumed by many to be objective truth and universally valid. This in turn allowed his successors to assume a mantle of sincerity in their *ex cathedra* pronouncements, even when their relationship to the truth was as tenuous as his own, as the ensuing chapters in this book will elucidate.

CHAPTER TWO

GUSTAV MAHLER'S *RESURRECTION* AND THE APOSTOLIC SUCCESSION

I t is one of the best-known epiphanies of the romantic era. Some five years after writing a vast movement for orchestra entitled "Todtenfeier" (Funeral rite), Gustav Mahler decided it should open his Second Symphony. He began work on the middle movements in the summer of 1893 but came to a halt at the finale, uncertain as to how to finish the thing. On February 12, 1894, Mahler's mentor Hans von Bülow died in Cairo, whither he had gone in hopes that the climate might repair his fragile health. It didn't, he died, and his body was embalmed and shipped home for the funeral that took place in the Great Michaeliskirche in Hamburg on March 29. Mahler had played the "Todtenfeier" for von Bülow back in 1891, and the sources tell us that the old man had hated it[1]—yet posthumously, he supposedly provided the inspiration for Mahler to complete the work. On February 17, 1897, nearly three years after the funeral, Mahler wrote as follows to the critic Arthur Seidl:

> I had back then borne within me for a long time the idea of introducing a choir in the last movement and only the worry that it might be regarded as a superficial imitation of Beethoven made me hesitate time and again! Then Bülow died and I attended his funeral service.—The mood in which I sat there, thinking of the departed, was wholly in the spirit of the work

Figure 2.1a. The program for the funeral of Hans von Bülow in the Great St. Michaeliskirche, Hamburg, March 29, 1894. Reproduced with permission from the Hamburg University Library.

J. S. Bach: Praeludium für Orgel.

(Herr Organist Burjam.)

J. S. Bach: Chor aus der Matthäus-Passion.

Wenn ich einmal soll scheiden,
So scheide nicht von mir!
Wenn ich den Tod soll leiden,
So tritt du dann herfür.
Wenn mir am allerbängsten,
Wird um das Herze sein,
So reiss' mich aus den Aengsten
Kraft deiner Angst und Pein.

(Die Bach-Gesellschaft unter Leitung des Herrn Director **Ad. Mehrkens**).

Vorlesungen aus der Heiligen Schrift.

(Herr Hauptpastor Behrmann.)

Gemeindegesang.

(Der Knaben-Chor der St. Michaelis - Kirche unter Leitung des
Herrn Cantor Hammer und die Gemeinde.

Aufersteh'n, ja aufersteh'n wirst du
        mein Staub, nach kurzer Ruh',
Unsterblich's Leben
        wird, der dich schuf, dir geben.
Hallelujah!

Wieder aufzublüh'n, werd' ich gesä't;
        der Herr der Erndte geht
und sammelt Garben
        uns ein, uns ein, die starben.
Hallelujah!

Tag des Dank's, der Freudenthränen Tag!
        du meines Gottes Tag!
wenn ich im Grabe
        genug geschlummert habe,
erweckst du mich.

Figure 2.1a.—*(continued)*

Gedenkrede.

(Herr Hauptpastor Behrmann.)

J. S. Bach: Chor aus der Johannes-Passion.

Ruht wohl, ihr teuren Gebeine,
Um die ich nicht mehr trostlos weine,
Ich weiss einst giebt der Tod mir Ruh'.

Nicht stets umschliesset mich die Gruft.
Einst wenn Gott, mein Erlöser, ruft,
Dann eil' auch ich verklärt dem Himmel zu.

(Die Bach-Gesellschaft).

Figure 2.1a.—*(concluded)*

Figure 2.1b. The program for the cremation ceremony of Hans von Bülow in the Ohlsdorf Crematorium, Hamburg, March 29, 1894. Reproduced with permission from the Hamburg University Library.

1. Heiliger Dankgesang an die Gottheit.

Choral in lydischer Tonart aus dem Streichquartett, op. 132
von **Beethoven.**

In Anlass der Feier für Männerchor gesetzt und mit Worten versehen
von Dr. Hermann Behn.

_____

Dankgesang.

So bringen wir zu letzter Rast
Den müden Leib, der nun verblasst.
Nach schwerem Kampf und herben Leid
Zu Friedens Ruh' in Ewigkeit.

Der immer strebend sich bemüht, —
Erlöset ward das edle Glied;
Genesung von des Lebens Noth
Gab gnädig ihm ein sanfter Tod.

Da ihm der letzte Schleier sank,
Erhebt den Geist in heil'gem Dank,
Zur Gottheit in des Lichtes Höh'n,
Die Feier würdig zu begeh'n!

_____

2. Gedenkworte.

Figure 2.1b.—*(continued)*

3. Litaney von **Schubert.**

Für Männerchor gesetzt von Capellmeister **W. Siohel.**

Litaney.

Ruh't in Frieden alle Seelen,
Die vollbracht ein langes Quälen,
Die vollendet süssen Traum,
Die zum lichten Aetherraum
  Sind geschieden, —
  Alle Seelen ruht in Frieden!

Und die nie der Sonne lachten,
Unterm Mond auf Dornen wachten,
Gott im reinen Himmelslicht
Einst zu sehn von Angesicht
  Ruht in Frieden!
  Alle Seelen ruht in Frieden!

Pohl & von Behren, Hamburg.

Figure 2.1b.—(concluded)

that I was carrying around within me.—Then the choir in the organ loft
intoned the Klopstock chorale "Auferstehn"!—it hit me like a lightning
bolt ["wie ein Blitz"] and everything stood before my soul, perfectly clear
and plain! The creative man waits for just this lightning bolt, this is the
"holy conception"![2]

Seidl published Mahler's letter in 1900, and it has ever since been regarded
as a key document in the composer's biography.[3]

For Mahler to recall a single moment with such precision three years
after it happened might seem to confirm the impact that von Bülow's funeral had made on him, thus underlining the truthfulness of his account.
On the other hand, if it was such a decisive moment in the history of his
latest and biggest work, one wonders why Mahler seems not to have mentioned it to any of his friends immediately after the event. It is true that
many of Mahler's letters are lost, but it is still odd that his letter to Seidl is
the only one known to offer any description of that "lightning bolt." Nor
do the detailed recollections of Natalie Bauer-Lechner, Mahler's assiduous
would-be Boswell of the mid-1890s, contain any mention of it.

The program booklet for von Bülow's funeral had printed the first three
stanzas of the Klopstock poem (see fig. 2.1a). Mahler took the first two as
the starting point for a choral finale to his symphony, adding a continuation of his own that elaborates the theme of resurrection and of soaring up
and away to God, though in a manner that avoids both the "hallelujahs"
found in Klopstock's original and any directly Christian terminology (this
was also, presumably, why Mahler did not use the third stanza as printed,
with its reference to "the day of my God").

Various commentators have discussed the genesis of the Second
Symphony's finale at length,[4] though the tale of Mahler's sudden inspiration
has been retold at face value in just about every book on him, probably because to doubt it would mean calling him at best a man economical with the
vérité.[5] That would be awkward; after all, Mahler had been raised to sainthood by Arnold Schoenberg on the dedication page of his *Harmonielehre* of
1911 (evidently taking his cue from Wagner's association of sainthood with
composing as discussed above),[6] and his halo henceforth received a proper
polishing from nearly everyone from Adorno on.[7] Mahler's "Klopstocking
moment" has even been commemorated by an elaborate plaque erected
in the Michaeliskirche by the Gustav Mahler Vereinigung, implicitly placing beyond the pale any doubts as to its veracity.[8] Yet by putting Mahler's
epiphany into its proper context, we can shed light not just on his Second
Symphony but also on his conducting career, his religion, and his relations

with both von Bülow and the man who for the next sixteen years would be his most powerful supporter and his principal rival.

There are two accounts by contemporaries that seem to confirm the content of Mahler's letter to Seidl. One is by his nephew Alfred Rosé (1902–75), the son of Mahler's sister Justine, in an article published and re-published in various German and Austrian newspapers in 1928 and 1929. Rosé presumably relied on family anecdote; he quotes several times from Mahler's letters to Justine, though he gets his facts wrong, claiming, for example, that Mahler conducted at the funeral. His account added no information that had not already been published elsewhere.[9] Nor did he offer any source (epistolary or otherwise) for his information on the event in the Michaeliskirche.

More interesting are the reminiscences of Mahler's friend Josef Foerster, who attended the funeral and who over a period of some thirty years offered variously elaborate versions in Czech and German of what happened. Foerster's wife Berta was an opera singer who was engaged under Mahler at the Hamburg Opera in mid-1893. According to Foerster himself, Mahler was so impressed with her command of the role of Eva at her first rehearsal for Wagner's *Meistersinger* that he asked to know who had trained her. When she replied that it was her husband, Mahler insisted on meeting him. Foerster relates how he and Mahler shared many musical opinions. Foerster was one of the early few to recognize his true greatness as a composer, and the two quickly became fast friends. Their intimacy is confirmed by Foerster's account of his presence at the epiphany of the Michaeliskirche. The earliest version that he published was in the Viennese journal *Der Merker* in the summer of 1910:

> A Prelude by J. S. Bach served as the introduction to the dignified commemoration and was followed by the chorus "Wenn ich einmal soll scheiden" from the *Matthew Passion*. Then the main pastor read from the Bible, and now the boys of the Michaeliskirche Choir began to sing Klopstock's "Auferstehn" with organ accompaniment. How the children's voices became the voices of angels, how deeply moved was the listening congregation, my words cannot tell: it was to me the most moving thing that I have ever experienced. It sounded like a proclamation of holy hope, it had the sanctified air of a prayer, the power of a miracle and the magic of a fairy tale [*Märchen*]. And as it sounded, all hearts sang along:
>
> Aufersteh'n, ja aufersteh'n wirst du
> [etc., Foerster quotes the first three stanzas as printed on the funeral program]

Then the old bells of the Michaeliskirche began their lament, as they had
bemoaned the loss of so many a dead man before, and their somber tones
lay like a thick mist over the city, filling it with grief.

I had not spoken to Mahler during the funeral. But in the afternoon I felt
an urge to visit him. As I opened the door of his simple study, he was sitting at his table. He turned and said: "Foerster, I have it." And I replied:
"Aufersteh'n, ja aufersteh'n." Then he looked at me, astonished and confused, for I had guessed his deepest secret.

   That is how the Finale of Gustav Mahler's Second Symphony came
about.[10]

As we can see from his many metaphors and similes, Foerster fancied
himself as a poetic essayist. While not all the articles he published on Mahler
featured the above tale (his obituary for the journal *Smetana* in 1911 has
not a hint of it),[11] wherever he did include it, the details varied. It is noteworthy that in September 1910, Paul Stefan published *Gustav Mahler: Eine
Studie über Persönlichkeit und Werk*, in which he briefly mentioned the
funeral of Bülow as having inspired the finale of the Second Symphony.[12]
His interviewees for the book had included Foerster and his wife, and since
Stefan (like everyone else) was familiar with the Mahler/Seidl account of
the moment in the Michaeliskirche, he must have asked Foerster about it.
Perhaps, by publishing "his" version of the story two months before Stefan,
Foerster was staking a claim to authenticity and making sure that his version was the first (since Mahler's own) to reach the public eye. That might
also explain the absence of the tale in his obituary of Mahler a year later, for
he by then would have felt no compulsion to prove or preempt anything.
   A decade after the piece in the *Merker*, Foerster published three articles of reminiscences of Mahler in *Smetana* (in Czech) and one in the
1920 Mahler issue of *Musikblätter des Anbruch* (in German). With regard
to the day in the Michaeliskirche, these correspond largely to what he had
previously written for the *Merker*, though they are rather more intricate
than the original. Oddly, in *Anbruch*, Foerster omits the detail of his inner
urge to visit Mahler and his guessing the latter's "deepest secret." He writes
instead that when he heard the Klopstock chorale in the church,

I too read the text and had in that same moment the feeling that also took
hold of Mahler: here was the Finale for the Second Symphony. On the
afternoon of the same day my premonition was confirmed and I found
Mahler already at work. When the Finale was finished and I shook the
hand of my friend, tears in my eyes, it struck us both that there was a gap

between the Scherzo and the last movement. Mahler then went into his treasure trove of older songs and . . . drew on "Urlicht."[13]

The most elaborate version of the story is the one in Foerster's autobiography, published when he was eighty (thus some forty-five years after the event). Gone are the holy hope and the fairy tales of the *Merker*; now he writes:

> In the afternoon [after the funeral] I wasn't at peace; as if driven by an order I hurried to him [Mahler]. I open the door and see him sitting at his desk, his head bowed down with a pen in his hand above the manuscript paper. I am still standing in the doorway. Mahler turns round and declares: "Friend, I have it!"
>
> I understood and as if enlightened by some mysterious power I reply: "Aufersteh'n, ja aufersteh'n wirst du nach kurzem Schlaf." In the greatest astonishment and surprise Mahler looks at me. I had guessed his secret, which he had not yet confided to a single human soul: Klopstock's poem, which that morning we had heard from the mouths of children, will form the basis of the final movement of his Second Symphony.[14]

(The shifts from past to present tense and back are all original).

In each case the moment of inspiration occasioned by hearing the Klopstock chorale really belongs to Foerster. In the version published in *Anbruch*, Foerster and Mahler shared a further inspirational moment by realizing that something was "missing" before the final movement. But this chronology for "Urlicht" is contrary to what we know for sure of the symphony's gestation. As Foerster should have realized, the music of the song is woven into that of the Finale itself, making it impossible for the former to have been an afterthought. Besides, Mahler finished the sketch of the final movement later that summer in his little composing house in Austria, far enough from Foerster for a handshake of any kind to have been a physical impossibility, let alone a tear-jerking friendly one. In a letter to his sister Justine, Mahler does mention playing the Second Symphony to Foerster (implying that it was for the first time), though this was not until September 1894, when the work was finished and "Urlicht" already embedded in it.[15]

If two aspects of Foerster's recollections are thus completely wrong, we would do well to take a closer look at his other claims. First we should question just how close Mahler and Foerster really were. They always remained on formal terms (a note sent by Mahler to Foerster as late as 1907 confirms that they still called each other "*Sie*"),[16] and while that was not unusual among friends in the society of the day, there are no documents apart from Foerster's reminiscences that suggest they ever became intimate. Mahler did call Foerster "an excellent musician and human being" in the abovementioned letter to Justine of September 1894, but since Foerster had just compared his Second Symphony with Beethoven's Ninth, this was probably not an objective appraisal.[17] A photo of Mahler exists from April 1897, signed "To my dear friend Josef Foerster," though it was a memento given when Mahler was about to leave Hamburg, so a certain degree of familiar sentiment was hardly surprising.[18] They had known each other for just a few months by the day of von Bülow's funeral, so we must wonder whether Mahler would really have confided in Foerster about the progress of a piece literally within minutes of beginning it. Besides, had they been such good friends, then they would surely have gone to the funeral together and sat together, which Foerster implies was not the case. Foerster's own reminiscences also make it clear that Mahler's departure from Hamburg in 1897 essentially signaled the end of whatever intimacy had hitherto existed between the two men, despite Foerster and his wife later following Mahler to Vienna.[19] We can assume that Mahler and Foerster were colleagues on good, everyday terms, but it was probably little more than that. A friendship as close as the one Foerster postulates rarely ceases as effortlessly as it seems theirs did.

There are two details in Foerster's final version that are telling, one geographical and the other chronological. He writes how he "hurried" to Mahler's apartment that same afternoon and "opens" the door to find him already at work—note his odd shift to the present tense, as if to reassure himself of the immediacy of the experience. But as Foerster himself mentioned elsewhere in his articles, when one reached Mahler's flat, one couldn't simply open the door and see the genius at his desk in the grip of inspiration. Guests were received at the door by Mahler's landlady (or a servant of hers) who then ushered them along a corridor into a room that led through another closed door into Mahler's study. Foerster here telescopes geographical, spatial reality. As for the chronology: it seems that Mahler was not even at home that afternoon. We know that he had to attend von Bülow's private cremation in Ohlsdorf after the main funeral because he there played the harmonium accompaniment to several singers from the City Theater in a choral arrangement of an excerpt from Beethoven's String Quartet op. 132 (see fig. 2.1b).[20] He had written to his sister Justine early that morning that "we will be funeralizing [*trauerfeiern*] from 9 in the morning until about 5 pm (at which time the funeral reception will be held at the Behns)."[21] Such a length of time is understandable, given that the hearse proceeded slowly through town after the funeral in order to be serenaded by instrumentalists gathered at the City Theater.[22] We cannot rule out the possibility that Mahler dashed home for a snack after the first service, but there was probably no time for it, and his letter to Justine implies that the obsequies were an all-day matter. The Ohlsdorf cemetery and crematorium lay some six miles from the center of the city, so it would have taken a while for the hearse to get there. Nor would Mahler's journey there and back have been much quicker, since Ohlsdorf was not connected to the city by an electric tramline until 1895. He presumably traveled with all the others, arriving back at the house of Franz Hermann and Luise Behn in time for the funeral meal at five in the afternoon. They lived at Oberstrasse 87, just under a mile from Mahler's flat on the Fröbelstrasse. Mahler would have been unable to dash away from the wake, for his position on Hamburg's music scene would have meant staying to indulge in the same polite small talk that his correspondence with his sister suggests he would rather have avoided. We can thus be sure that he did not manage to get home during the day. Even more damning for Foerster's reliability is the fact that the extant sources show that Mahler conducted Smetana's *Bartered Bride* at 7:00 p.m. in the City Theater that same evening (in fact, Foerster's wife was singing the title role).[23]

The theater bill listing Mahler as the conductor was published either on the day of the performance or the day before,[24] so unless he spontaneously and surreptitiously handed over the direction of the evening to a deputy, unnoticed and unremarked upon afterward by the critics, he would have had a window of just a few minutes in which to arrive back from the Behns, sit at his desk, sketch out his finale, and be observed doing so by Foerster before dashing off to conduct Smetana. In fact, Mahler quite possibly kept his concert clothes at the theater and did not even go home at all between the Behns and the *Bride*. We have little option but to conclude that Mahler was not at home that afternoon, that he did not sit at his desk to work on his Second Symphony or anything else that day, and that Foerster's reminiscences are a complete fabrication.

Bernd Schabbing has already drawn attention to various minor errors in Foerster's articles on Mahler (such as writing "Bereut" instead of "Bernuth"), and although these might in any other context be dismissed as typesetting errors beyond the author's control, they do fit the pattern of general inaccuracy that we have charted here.[25] Since Foerster's recollections become more elaborate as the years go by, with certain details coming and going, we must suppose that this process of fictional elaboration, either by design or error, had already begun by the time he wrote for the *Merker* in 1910. We can give

Figure 2.2. The Hamburg theater bill for 29 March 1894, listing Mahler as conductor. Courtesy of Universität Hamburg, Hamburger Theatersammlung.

Foerster the benefit of the doubt and postulate that he was not consciously lying, but that at some point in the months after von Bülow's funeral he may indeed have visited Mahler as he was working on his choral finale. Events at a distance of sixteen years can in retrospect seem closer together than ever they were in reality (and they can get even more confused up to forty years after the event). Foerster's use of the word *Märchen* (fairy tale) in his *Merker* article might well have been a Freudian slip that betrays what his conscious mind refused to admit, for "fairy tale" is used in German, as in English, to denote something one might wish were true, but isn't. Mahler's letter to Seidl had long been published and its contents known to all and sundry (Foerster actually refers to it specifically in his later *Anbruch* article), so the composer's own telling could have merged with Foerster's recollections to the extent that Mahler's moment of inspiration at some point became, to Foerster, a joint one. The fact that they both write of only the choir singing the Klopstock hymn is also an odd commonality that does not fit with the objective truth, for it was sung by the whole congregation—some thousand people altogether, including Mahler and Foerster—with the boy's choir in the organ loft merely taking the lead. It seems most likely that Foerster's recollection was colored by already having read Mahler's account (and if anything of the funeral service did find its way into the Second Symphony, then it was perhaps the low murmuring of the congregation that is usual as a hymn gets underway, for the effect is not dissimilar to the muted entrance of the chorus in Mahler's last movement).

Foerster would not have been the first to exaggerate the closeness of his relationship with a great man (note also that "Foerster, I have it" in 1910 becomes the more intimate "Friend, I have it" thirty years later). Since their friendship had dwindled after Hamburg, Foerster's account perhaps compensated for an absence of actual intimacy by conjuring it up in retrospect. By claiming that he had acknowledged Mahler's composing genius at a time when almost no one else had done so, Foerster's praise of him also became self-reflecting. He probably needed it: since those days in Hamburg, Mahler—younger than Foerster by a year—had become world famous, while Foerster's reputation as a composer and teacher remained quite local. Who could blame him for bending the truth?

If Foerster's reminiscences must now be regarded as of dubious authenticity and dependent on Mahler's own, how reliable is Mahler himself? There is nothing in Mahler's extant letters to his sister Justine after March 29, 1894, to suggest that anything happened in the Michaeliskirche except the funeral itself. He did write to her the next day, but only with career news—he had heard the night before that his chances of taking on some of von Bülow's concerts had dramatically increased.[26] Since he often wrote to her of matters specific to his composing, he would surely have told her of any epiphany in the church before confiding it to Foerster or another outsider. But he did not. As mentioned above, what Mahler wrote to Seidl in 1897 seems to have been the first written or oral account that he gave to anyone of his inspirational moment. But why Seidl? The two had become acquainted when Seidl wrote a positive review of Ernst von Schuch's performance of the three middle movements of Mahler's Second Symphony in Dresden on January 15, 1897. Mahler's success as a composer had thus far been negligible, so Seidl's praise was manna from heaven. Mahler made this clear when he wrote to thank Seidl on January 21, 1897, a letter in which he mentions that the piano score of his Second Symphony has already been forwarded to him. Seidl was three years younger than Mahler and a rising star in German music circles. He had been a vociferous Wagnerian when a student, had published his university thesis on aesthetics in 1887 (*Vom Musikalisch-Erhabenen*), and in 1892 had published a book entitled *Hat Richard Wagner eine Schule hinterlassen?* (*Did Richard Wagner bequeath a "school"?*) Significantly, Seidl was an old friend of Richard Strauss, whom he had first met in Munich in the 1880s, and with whom he had discussed everything from Schopenhauer to Nietzsche. Seidl was also the principal author of the first book (a slim one) to be published on Strauss, which had appeared in 1896, not long before Seidl praised Mahler in print.[27]

Mahler's letter to Seidl is unusually long and detailed, considering that he was writing to a virtual stranger. It offers high praise for Strauss, making it clear that Mahler already recognized him as his most significant peer. The praise is justified, though it was also judicious to include it, given that Strauss and Seidl were close friends. For Mahler to write such an elaborate, carefully confessional tract to a man he barely knew, but who had just brought out a book on his main rival, there can only be one reasonable explanation: Mahler wanted Seidl to write about him *too*, and this letter was meant for publication. The score of the Second Symphony had just been published, so offering information about it would have been a hefty nudge to Seidl to write about the work. Mahler was making sure that if Seidl followed through, his interpretation of the work would in effect be the one that Mahler desired. Seidl did indeed publish the letter, though not for another three years, by which time Mahler seems to have taken little joy in its publication (or at least pretended so).[28] After this, the story of Mahler's stroke of inspiration at von Bülow's funeral soon gained general currency.

One matter that is particularly striking about the content of Mahler's letter is its repeated use of Christian terminology. Thus Mahler searched "all of world literature down to the Bible in order to find the word of sal-vation"; his moment of inspiration was "the holy conception" [*das heilige Empfängnis*]; and when he writes of Strauss's aims being similar to his own, he calls it "signs and wonders" (see Romans 15:19) that point to a future victory for them both. Just six days later, Mahler would convert to Roman Catholicism. His choice of words here raises certain questions, though: if he was searching for a word of salvation, why did he implicitly consult the Bible last (unless, of course, it was merely a means to an end and of little real spiritual significance to him)? And why write of a "*hei-liges Empfängnis*"? While the phrase does occur in German-language cat-echisms of the nineteenth century,[29] it is not a concept generally referred to in the Catholic tradition, which in the case of Christ's conception speaks of "*Mariä Verkündigung*," the Annunciation. The feast of *Mariä Empfängnis*, on the other hand, is that of the "immaculate conception," the idea that Mary herself was conceived without original sin. Was Mahler merely twist-ing Catholic vocabulary to suit his own ends?

Mahler's conversion took place in the main Catholic church in cen-tral Hamburg, the "Kleine" Michaeliskirche, which stood a mere stone's throw from the "Grosse" Michaeliskirche, the Protestant church where von Bülow's funeral had taken place. Mahler was at the time hoping for a post at the Vienna State Opera, which he knew would be impossible for him to attain if he remained Jewish. So it was in his interest to utilize Christian vocabulary in a letter that he presumably hoped would be published, for it could help to underline his Christian credentials at a crucial time. More to the point, Arthur Seidl wrote for the anti-Semitic press in Germany (he had become the editor of the cultural section of the nationalist *Deutsche Wacht* in Dresden in 1893).[30] Perhaps Mahler thought that if he could get men such as Seidl on his side and convince them of his commitment to Christianity, then anti-Semitic opposition to him might dwindle. His oth-er, extensive correspondence at this time leaves no doubt that he was aware that his Jewishness would hinder his career, and that he took all possible steps to lessen its impact. He had already endeavored to get the sympathy of the Wagner family and inveigled anyone and everyone to help him get the Viennese appointment he so desired. He specifically mentioned the influence of "the anti-Semitic papers" in a letter to Ludwig Karpath of April 11, 1897.[31] But, as has been remarked by Eveline Nikkels, Mahler's letter to Seidl also contains several references to Nietzsche's writings, in particular to the description in *Ecce homo* of the moment of artistic inspiration that is "like a lightning bolt," [*wie ein Blitz*][39]—the same phrase that Mahler used. It is hardly an original simile (as mentioned in the introduction, Arthur

Koestler's *Act of Creation* offers a host of other examples of its use), but given the context, the reference was probably intentional. Mahler knew that Seidl was a dedicated Nietzschean (Seidl even joined the staff of the Nietzsche Archives a year later), and it is noteworthy that Mahler in his letter repeats the word *Blitz*—"lightning bolt"—just a line or two after its first mention, as if to make sure that Seidl would take note of it.

These are not the only references in the letter. Constantin Floros has remarked that certain passages in it are virtual paraphrases of passages from Wagner's essay on Beethoven, while the description of the creative musician as "like a sleepwalker" [*wie ein Nachtwandler*] is reminiscent of both Wagner and Schopenhauer (the simile is one that the former knew from the latter, and used repeatedly in "Beethoven" in 1870).[33] Mahler might even be thinking of Wagner's stroke of inspiration in La Spezia (although the lengthy version best known today only became common knowledge after the first publication of *Mein Leben* in 1911, a truncated one had already been published in Wagner's "Letter to an Italian friend about the performance of *Lohengrin* in Bologna" in volume 9 of his complete writings in 1873).[34] The wording of Mahler's letter would appear to have been intended to kill several birds with one stone, namely to convince Seidl—friend of Strauss; confirmed Schopenhauerian, Nietzschean, and Wagnerian; and a representative of the anti-Semitic press—that Mahler was Christian, appreciative of Strauss, and in every way wholly in tune with Seidl's own Germanocentric, musico-philosophical attitudes.

Our interpretation of Mahler's letter as primarily an example of self-propaganda is further underlined by its closing, where he apologizes for writing "in great haste in the middle of preparations for a tour of several weeks that will take me to Moscow, Petersburg, Munich, Budapest, etc." Nothing about the letter reads hurried. Quite apart from its complex web of references to the writings of Nietzsche, Wagner, and Schopenhauer, Mahler would hardly have had the time to drop the names of all the cities he was to visit, had he really been so rushed. But it does sound impressive, making him out to be a man everywhere in demand.

For us to suggest that Mahler was eager to win over Seidl might seem to be reading too much into too little, for Seidl was still only in his thirties and hardly had the public clout of, say, a Hanslick. Nor did he have intimate connections in Vienna that could have been of immediate help to Mahler in his eagerness to get a big job there. But Mahler was at the same time hoping for the directorship of the Kaim Orchestra in Munich, Seidl's native city—the same city where Seidl's friend Strauss was working at the Opera. Journalists who liked Mahler's music were as yet rare beasts, and since Mahler needed all the friends he could get, it must have made sense to court Seidl (not that it did much good, as Mahler's concert in March with the Kaim Orchestra was not a success, and he did not get the job).[35] While from our perspective, Seidl might not seem a big fish, from Mahler's perspective he probably seemed much bigger.

Mahler's reminiscences are thus hardly more reliable than Foerster's, though they were written with a different purpose, and their imagery—including that bolt of lightning—pilfered from elsewhere. It seems to have been generally overlooked that the text of Klopstock's "Auferstehung" was almost certainly known to Mahler before von Bülow's funeral. It had been published in Klopstock's *Geistliche Lieder* in 1758 and thereafter set to music by Carl Heinrich Graun, Carl Philipp Emanuel Bach, and others. Over the ensuing decades it was printed in Protestant hymnbooks all across Germany (including Klopstock's own Hamburg homeland) and became a regular feature at funerals. It was presumably included at von Bülow's not because of any known affinity for it on the part of the deceased, but because it was the thing to sing at such occasions, just like the other musical numbers on the program—Bach's "Wenn ich einmal soll scheiden" from the *Saint Matthew Passion* and his "Ruhet wohl" from the *Saint John*. Besides, "Auferstehung" would hardly have been included as the only congregational hymn, had those organizing the event imagined it was so unknown that no one would be able to sing along. While Mahler was not yet "officially" a Christian and thus no regular churchgoer, he would hardly have been able to live his life in complete ignorance of one of the standard funeral hymns by one of Germany's best-known writers. So any element of "eureka" upon coming across Klopstock's poem at the funeral can probably be discounted. It is also possible that Mahler knew beforehand what was to be sung at von Bülow's funeral—after all, he had to play at the cremation, so he might have asked or been told of the musical program for the rest of the day. What if Mahler had learned that the Klopstock was to be sung and even anticipated in advance the possibility that it might "inspire" him? It is hardly more improbable than the tale that he offered Seidl.

There is a further aspect of the reception of Klopstock's hymn that is of particular interest. For Mahler was not even the first composer to be "inspired" by it. In 1814, Schubert had set a poem by Friedrich von Matthisson entitled "An Laura, als sie Klopstock's Auferstehungslied sang" (To Laura, when she sang Klopstock's resurrection song," i.e., his "Auferstehung"). This song (D 115) is a celebration in words and music of the act of being inspired by Klopstock's text. Since it had been published in 1840 (in Diabelli's thirteenth volume of Schubert's *Nachlass*) it is reasonable to assume that

Mahler knew it too—for his intimate knowledge of Schubert is evident from his own vocal oeuvre. And there is an interesting parallel between Matthisson's text and Mahler's continuation of Klopstock, for in both, the narrator speaks of how he will "soar away" [entschweben], up toward the light of God.

To this web of references to Wagner, Nietzsche, Schopenhauer, and now Schubert, we must add one more name. Eveline Nikkels has postulated that Mahler's text was influenced by the words of Brahms's *German Requiem*, the first two movements of which had been performed at the concert in memory of von Bülow held on February 26, 1894 (and at which Mahler had himself conducted Beethoven's *Eroica* Symphony). Nikkels points out in particular the similarities between Mahler's program for his last movement and the sixth movement of the Brahms, with its last judgment, the last trump, and resurrection.[36] The most striking similarity, however, is not between Mahler's text and the Brahms, but between the text of Brahms's first movement and the second strophe of Klopstock with their common images of "sowing," "harvest," and "sheaves." The fact that Brahms's Requiem avoids directly Christian references might also have suggested to Mahler the idea of doing something similar in his symphony, hence his having kept only Klopstock's first two verses. By February 1897, however, when his Jewishness risked jeopardizing his future career, the lack of religious specificity in his Second Symphony could have counted against him. His letter to Seidl, with its overtly Christian terminology, can thus be interpreted as an attempt to reverse the "de-Christianization" to which he had subjected Klopstock at the time. Besides, as Mahler would have known, Seidl was a vehement anti-Brahmsian. If he had indeed taken the *German Requiem* as a model in any way, it was something best kept to himself.

Pace Foerster, there are no sketches for the finale that can be proven to date from the day of the funeral, nor even from the immediate weeks thereafter. And as has been remarked by numerous commentators, the chorale tune to which Klopstock's words were usually sung bears no resemblance to Mahler's setting, though this might have been expected, had the singing of it truly brought about that "lightning bolt" of which he wrote. It would not be impossible for a musical experience—hearing the Klopstock hymn—to prompt a composer to write, spontaneously, a completely different music to the same text, though it would seem a little odd. Stephen Hefling has identified an early sketch for Mahler's continuation of Klopstock's text, written on the back of a letter sent to him by his sister Justine dated "Rome, 28.4."[37] A further, more elaborate stage in the gestation of the text for the final movement is dated "Steinbach, Mitwoch [*sic*], 13 Juni 1894" (Steinbach, Wednesday, June 13, 1894), though even here the text has not yet reached its final form, for the last stanza repeats Klopstock's "mein Staub, nach kurzer Ruh," which Mahler later amended to "Mein Herz, in einem Nu." Hefling has examined all the extant sketches for the movement,[38] one of which is of the opening music of Mahler's Klopstock setting (and as yet without his added text) and was presumably the first musical sketch for the chorus. It is, however, undated. A letter exists from Mahler to Arnold Berliner, postmarked June 15, 1894, in which he announces that he has "begun" work, referring, undoubtedly, to the symphony's finale. In fact, no one but Foerster has ever suggested that Mahler began work on his finale on the day of von Bülow's funeral—not even Mahler claimed that, though his "lightning bolt" in his letter to Seidl implies it. To judge by the admittedly sparse sources available, he did not begin it until several weeks later.

This is all well and good. We can deconstruct as many accounts of von Bülow's funeral as we like, explore all possible influences and call the veracity of all words and memories into question, but in the end we are still faced with the undeniable fact that it was Klopstock's "Aufersteh'n," one of the songs sung at von Bülow's funeral, that Mahler not long afterward took as the basis for the choral finale of his Second Symphony. The relative chronological proximity of the funeral and the act of composition (two-and-a-half months at most) does suggest the likelihood of some causal connection. Because Mahler held von Bülow in high regard, we can imagine that he took the funeral program home with him and put it on his desk, meaning that he had Klopstock's text to hand for as long as it lay there. So perhaps closer to the truth than any Nietzschean lightning bolt would be a reading in which Mahler, either during or after the funeral—or even before it—was struck (consciously or no) by the textual echoes of Klopstock in the Brahms Requiem. This in turn, we propose, was fused with a memory of Schubert's song in which Klopstock's text acts as a prompt for both poetic and musical inspiration.

In his book *The Haunting Melody*, which is quoted in much of the literature on the Second Symphony, the psychologist Theodore Reik (one of Freud's students) posited that Mahler's inspiration at von Bülow's funeral was intimately bound up with a subconscious "death wish" that he had borne toward the man who had condemned his "Todtenfeier" movement at its private hearing. Reik suggests that it was von Bülow's death and his own subsequent "Totenfeier" that removed Mahler's supposed block, allowing him to complete the symphony.[39] He draws on the content of Mahler's letter to Seidl, though his interpretation is not dependent on it. So while the web of influences we postulate above might have provided the fodder for the choral finale of his Second Symphony, if any one event did trigger the completion of the work, then it was not just von Bülow's funeral, but his death and the whole conglomeration of emotions that it must have called forth—for the absence of von Bülow, while cause for sorrow, also meant prospects of advancement. As Mahler himself mentioned in his above-mentioned letter to Justine, von Bülow's subscription concerts were now up for grabs (though when Mahler took on von Bülow's Hamburg series in the next season, it was not a success).

We can revisit Mahler's letter to Seidl in the light of Reik's analysis in order to draw a farther-reaching conclusion. If we accept that there was *some* causal connection between von Bülow's death and the conclusion of Mahler's Second Symphony, albeit as a convoluted reaction to sudden freedom from a quasi-parental authority, then it also makes sense to conclude that Mahler's letter to Seidl still reverberates with that reaction, reducing it to a single moment that probably never happened—that "lightning bolt" or "holy conception." The insistent references to Richard Strauss, intended superficially to endear Mahler to Seidl, as postulated above, are also an act of recognition that Strauss is Mahler's biggest rival: as composer, as conductor, and as heir to the musical traditions that they shared. Let us replace Mahler's religious metaphor with another, similar one: by saying that he received inspiration from on high at the funeral of Hans von Bülow (a "holy conception" means being penetrated by the Holy Ghost), Mahler is laying claim to the "Apostolic Succession" of the Austro-German tradition. Von Bülow was not just the champion of Brahms and Wagner but the son-in-law of Liszt, who in turn (according to nineteenth-century legend) had received a "kiss of benediction" from Beethoven, who in *his* turn (in the words of Count Waldstein) had gone to Vienna to "receive the spirit of Mozart from Haydn's hands." If he did not know it before, then Mahler will have been made aware of the concept of the Apostolic Succession while being prepared for his conversion to Roman Catholicism, and he could have expected a man such as Seidl, brought up as he was in the Catholic state of Bavaria, to have understood the allusion. Mahler's occasional self-identification with Beethoven has been noted by other commentators, and as James L. Zychowicz has pointed out, the musicological interest in Beethoven's sketches in the late nineteenth century seems to have prompt-ed Mahler to destroy most of his own sketches in order that his creative process might not be investigated after the same fashion. As Zychowicz remarks, "No full set of sketches exists for any single work" of Mahler's.[40] One might also add that destroying the traces of his creative process also enabled Mahler to impose his own interpretations of his work more easily (if there were a dated sketchbook for the final movement of the Second Symphony, it would have been easy enough to prove or disprove the stories that built up surrounding its conception).

Mahler's rivalry with Strauss was nothing new. It must even at times have seemed to Mahler as if the younger man was dogging his footsteps wherever he went. Mahler had wanted to work with von Bülow back in 1884, but had been rejected. Soon thereafter, von Bülow had appointed Strauss as his assistant instead.[41] There had been a threat that Mahler might be ousted in Hamburg to make way for Strauss in early 1894;[42] and although they had both since then written huge works based on Nietzsche's *Zarathustra*, Mahler's Third Symphony remained as yet unperformed, while Strauss's *Also sprach* had received its successful first performance on November 27, 1896, just weeks before Mahler wrote to Seidl. As Mahler knew, von Bülow had died in Cairo because Strauss had recommended to him the therapeutic qualities of its climate. While it must have been clear to everyone that von Bülow was by then beyond any therapy at all, Mahler might in some respect have blamed Strauss for his death. Strauss had been due to conduct the Hamburg subscription concert on February 26 that was turned into the von Bülow commemoration, but he had pulled out when the organizers refused his program suggestions. That had allowed Mahler to step in. As his letters prove, the impact of his conducting at such a high-profile event seems to have done much for his reputation outside Hamburg. If in life von Bülow had preferred Strauss over him, then the letter to Seidl was Mahler's chance to wrest back von Bülow's blessing, posthumously. The near-certainty that Strauss would learn of the letter (through Seidl personally, if not in print) was perhaps what allowed Mahler to praise him so highly in it, for now he could prove that at the end, even beyond the grave, he had been von Bülow's favored one. And since von Bülow was dead, there was no one around to contradict Mahler's version of events. This, too, could offer us a reason why Mahler—who had no doubt learned his Catholic theology well—should have written of a "holy conception" instead of an "immaculate" one. An immaculate conception would have made him without sin; and in a letter that almost certainly breaks the ninth and tenth commandments by bearing false witness and coveting his neighbor's success, Mahler might on some level of his subconscious have reckoned that any claim to spotlessness on his part would have been decidedly shaky.

If the claim to authenticity of that plaque in the Michaeliskirche is now shaky too, the broader truth behind it remains not unconvincing. Were it not for the one "Todtenfeier," the other might not have reached the conclusion that it did. But the "Auferstehung" of which Mahler's text speaks is really that of his own symphony, a work that had been declared dead or dying by von Bülow, and which rose up to completion only after von Bülow's death.

CHAPTER THREE

OF FORKED TONGUES AND ANGELS

Alban Berg's Violin Concerto

*My Almschi, I don't know when I will see you, nor whether I will
be able to express what is unspeakable—if only in a wordless
embrace. Nor do I wish to attempt in a letter to find words
where language fails. . . . And yet: one day—before this terrible
year is at an end—a score will be dedicated
to the memory of an angel
that might express, in sounds, to you and Franz
what I feel and that I can find no words to express today.*

Your Alban

—Letter from Alban Berg to Alma Mahler-Werfel, ca. May 1935

H ere are the facts as given, virtually uncontested, throughout the literature. Commissioned in February 1935 to write a concerto for the Ukrainian-American violinist Louis Krasner, Berg found the project at first intractable. Tragedy provided the inspiration that he needed when on April 22, 1935, Alma Mahler's eighteen-year-old daughter Manon Gropius died of polio. Work proceeded quickly thereafter, and the concerto was finished the following August.[1] But as he was putting the final touches to the full score— with its title-page dedication "To the memory of an angel" [Dem Angedenken eines Engels] as promised—Berg was stung by an insect. His health deteriorated, blood poisoning set in, and he died on December 24, 1935. Berg's pupil

Willi Reich had already told the story of the Violin Concerto's genesis and Manon's role in it in early autumn 1935, in an article written with the composer's collaboration (as Reich himself confirmed)[2] and published variously in the *Neues Wiener Journal*, *Anbruch*, and the *Schweizerische Musikzeitung* (Reich added further detail two years later in his book-length study of Berg). The version of the article published in *Anbruch* was entitled "Requiem for Manon," making its inspiration as evident as could be.[3] After Berg's early death, the concerto was soon seen by many as a requiem for the composer himself. Inevitably, comparisons were made with the Requiem by Mozart, long seen in the literature as that composer's own farewell to the world.

The story of Berg's Concerto is one of the most powerful tales of musical inspiration to emerge in the first half of the twentieth century: the death of a child prompting a composer to write a work that became his own monument. However, the tale becomes less straightforward when one examines the sources more carefully, and this enables us to explore more far-reaching correlations between Berg the man and Berg the constructivist composer than have hitherto been documented. The precise course of Berg's work on the concerto—just when he composed what of it—remains oddly vague, with some commentators maintaining that the commission was conveyed as early as autumn 1934.[4] Berg actually wrote to Krasner on March 28, 1935, to tell him that he had already made "all kinds of preliminary work" for it [*allerhand Vorarbeiten*]. As Douglas Jarman remarks in the introduction to his edition of the work in the Berg Complete Edition, the format of the work was by this date already determined to a large degree—nearly a month before Manon's death—even down to the incorporation of a set of chorale variations (though the melody for them had not yet been decided upon).[5]

Manon Gropius herself remains a shadowy figure of whom little is known except that she lived, she died, and her "angelicness" inspired the composer. The research of the past decades has not done much to clarify Manon's role in the work's genesis. In his sketches, Berg wrote "Lähmungsakkord" (chord of paralysis) at the climactic chord of the Allegro in the second half of the Concerto (*Kinderlähmung* is German for "polio"). The words *Stöhnen* (groaning) and *Seufzer* (sighs) there may also have referred to Manon's fate.[6] But there are many aspects of the work that do not seem to relate to Manon at all. For instance, Douglas Jarman, Constantin Floros, and others have discerned the repeated use of the numbers 23 and 10 and their multiples in all aspects of the Concerto, from the structure (e.g., the length of part 2, namely 230 measures) to the metronome markings (e.g., for part 2, 69 = 3 x 23), and while this was a consistent practice in all of Berg's music from the *Lyric Suite* onward, the number 23 was one he associated with himself, and the number 10 with Hanna Fuchs-Robettin, his lover since 1925. (Hanna was Franz Werfel's sister and thus Manon's step-aunt). Furthermore, the wistfully yodeling Carinthian folk song used prominently by Berg in the Concerto has been revealed to be more than a little ribald.[7] Entitled "Ein Vogel auf'm Zwetschgenbaum"—"A bird in the plum tree"—it tells of a boy in his girlfriend's bed who is awakened by the twittering of a bird outside at an early hour, and so slips out in time without being discovered. Douglas Jarman has postulated convincingly that this song might be a reference to the serving girl Marie Scheuchl with whom Berg had fathered a child when he was just seventeen. And if matters were not already complicated enough, Berg seems at the start briefly to have envisaged another "program" of sorts for the Concerto, basing its four movements on the words *frisch, fromm, fröhlich, frei* (fresh, pious, happy, free)— the motto of the German Gymnastics Association.[8] All this leaves Manon remarkably unreferred-to, though attempts have been made (with limited success) to identify the structural use of numbers that might or might not have some connection to her, too, such as the date of her death, 22.[9]

The exact cause and course of Berg's own illness, while the subject of much scholarly investigation, also remain opaque. Some sources say there was a bee sting, others a wasp sting, yet others a gnat bite, and everyone wonders whether his wife Helene really lanced his boil with her scissors and, if she did, whether this was what finally killed him.[10] Another oddity is the recollection of Berg's widow, conveyed "again and again" to Louis Krasner, of how Alban, "ill in bed and tortured with pain, worked frantically and without interruption to conclude the composition of his Violin Concerto. Refusing to stop for food or sleep, he drove his hand relentlessly and in fever. 'I must continue,' Berg responded to his wife's pleadings, 'I cannot stop—I do not have time.'"[11] But as stated above, Berg had already finished the work at roughly the same time in August that he experienced the sting or bite that would kill him four months later. Helene's implication that he somehow foresaw his death as he worked on the concerto is nicely poetic, but her own invention.

Before we tease apart the web of references that commentators have found in Berg's Violin Concerto, let us offer a further thread to it. By necessity, one of the earliest compositional ideas for the work was its note row, which is based around the violin's open strings. With its chains of thirds and obvious tonal references, it is one of the most oft-quoted rows in the literature. Berg himself wrote to Schoenberg of this row in a letter of August 28, 1935. To judge from his published correspondence, this was the first time since his *Lyric Suite* nine years earlier that he had notified his former teacher of a row he was using:

For my part I can report to you that the Violin Concerto has been finished for fourteen days already. . . .

For the whole thing, I've chosen a very fortunate row (since D major and other similar "violin concerto" keys are out of the question), namely:[12]

which by chance also yielded the beginning of the Bach chorale

"Es ist genug"

Berg might have quoted this row because it reflected with uncanny accuracy something that had preoccupied his teacher two years earlier. On February 12, 1933, Schoenberg had given a lecture on Frankfurt Radio that later, in its Americanized form, became known as "Brahms the Progressive." The occasion for the lecture was the centenary of the birth of Brahms, though Schoenberg gave it three months before the actual anniversary, on the eve of the fiftieth anniversary of Wagner's death instead. This was no matter of chance, for his avowed intent was a provocative redrawing of the boundaries of the "progressive" in music in order to place Brahms and Wagner on a more equal footing (with Schoenberg and his "school" implicitly as the true heirs of both). Schoenberg wanted, he said, "to recognize the true connection that exists between them; [to see] to what extent both were progressive musicians and academicians, fantasists, and formalists."[13] This lecture has achieved iconic status, with even its English title becoming a catchphrase to be quoted, copied, queried, and parodied in numerous essays since. One of the music examples that Schoenberg used in his lecture was taken from Brahms's Fourth Symphony. His script reads as follows:

> If one also considers that Wagner's leitmotif technique essentially represents an attempt to unify the thematic material of a whole opera, indeed of a whole tetralogy, then this is once more a purely formalistic intention, just as Brahms undertakes in no more of a formalist manner, e.g., in his E-minor symphony, when in the final movement he deploys the thirds of the first.[14]

descending   ascending: Inversion

Schoenberg omits to mention here that the fourth and final movement of the Brahms is a passacaglia based on a fragment taken from Bach's Cantata no. 150 (and the "deployment" to which he refers is to be found in measures 233–36, as he later made clear in the revised, English version). Brahms's source had been common knowledge for several years, while the passacaglia itself seems to have featured in Schoenberg's composition classes for even longer. Webern's Passacaglia op. 1, for example, was obviously modeled to a large degree on the last movement of Brahms's Fourth Symphony.[15]

Of interest to us here is that chain of interlocking major and minor thirds to which Schoenberg reduced the opening of the Brahms symphony. There is an undoubted similarity between Schoenberg's reduction of Brahms's theme and Berg's note row. In both works, the opening statement of the row/theme is followed by its inversion (measures 1–4 and 5–9 of the Brahms, as Schoenberg's above example illustrates, and measures 15–18 and 24–27 in the Berg). In each case, too, the theme/row is a horizontal delineation of its (vertical) accompanying harmony. To use a chain of thirds (ascending or descending) as the thematic basis for a movement was hardly new; Raymond Knapp observed that the opening of Mozart's Symphony no. 40 is constructed thus, and in his edition of Beethoven's sketches, Gustav Nottebohm showed that Beethoven had thought of using a chain of thirds for the opening of his Fifth Symphony.[16] When one considers, however, that the correlations between Brahms's Fourth Symphony and Berg's concerto do not begin and end with a chain of thirds, then they begin to seem less a matter of chance and more one of design. For each work also closes with a set of variations on a theme taken from a Bach cantata, which theme is then (as Schoenberg pointed out with regard to the Brahms) combined with the chain of thirds that was first stated in the opening movement.

Berg seems to have planned to use a chorale in his second movement right from the start. He had already incorporated a set of chorale variations in his opera *Lulu*, though in the present case he was quite possibly influenced by the second movement of Beethoven's Violin Concerto, where the accompanying texture is often in four parts and even resembles a chorale when the violin is accompanied by clarinets and bassoons (see ex. 3.1; Berg uses four clarinets to play his chorale for the first time). Berg first tried constructing a chorale melody himself from his chosen tone row (see ex. 3.2). This invented chorale is reminiscent of the opening of the Ricercare from Bach's *Musical Offering*, which Anton von Webern had just orchestrated and was about to conduct for the first time on April 25, 1935. So perhaps that work was on Berg's mind, or perhaps he later spotted the similarity and discarded his chorale for that reason. In any case, Willi Reich's assertion that Berg only decided on the use of Bach's chorale "Es ist genug" from Cantata no. 60 at a later stage in the compositional process—in June 1935—is generally accepted as accurate.[17] This would tie in with Berg's remark on his tone row in the abovementioned letter to Schoenberg of August 1935 that its last notes "by chance also yielded the beginning of the Bach chorale 'Es ist genug.'" As Achim Fiedler has pointed out, this chorale was not completely unknown to Berg, for he had attended a performance of the Cantata no. 60 in Vienna in 1914. It is a peculiar coincidence that, according to the scholarship of Berg's day, this cantata was believed to have been composed in 1732 for performance on November 23—the number that Berg regarded as so significant to his own person.[18]

Berg's variations in his second movement have always been regarded as "chorale variations," which one might suppose to be quite different in form from Brahms's passacaglia (sometimes described as a "chaconne"). Yet they are alike in that they both treat their theme as a cantus firmus that is sounded in different registers—at times in the bass, at others in the treble—though Berg allows himself the use of inversion and various transpositions. The Bach chorale chosen by Berg actually serves to emphasize the (otherwise superficial) similarity between the last, stepwise notes of his row and the theme of the Brahms passacaglia. As it happens, the first appearance of "Es ist genug" as a bass line in the Berg (at the beginning of the second variation) is in the very transposition (on E) that makes the proximity to the theme of Brahms's fourth movement apparent (and at which the second violins play an accompaniment figure whose rhythm is also to be found in the upper strings in one of Brahms's variations—this time probably coincidentally—namely in bar 153 of the symphony's last movement). One could even interpret Berg's row as a stylized, composite version of the chain of thirds from Brahms's first movement plus the stepwise ascending passacaglia theme from the fourth (see exx. 3.3 and 3.4).

While we can be sure that Berg knew Schoenberg's lecture (apart from the fact that broadcasts from Frankfurt could be heard as far away as Vienna, Berg asked specifically for a paper copy of it), there is no known record of Berg having based his row intentionally on Brahms.[19] Nor are the two composers' chains of thirds identical, for Berg begins with a minor third, Brahms with a major third. However, it is of interest that the pivotal note in Berg's row—the point at which his thirds stop (or at which they go retrograde) is a B♮, the same note with which Brahms's chain of thirds begins.

Example 3.1. Beethoven, Violin Concerto op. 61, second movement, mm. 71–76.

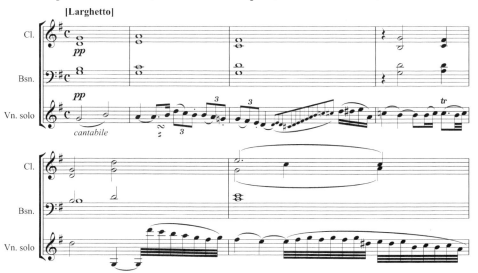

Example 3.2. The opening of Berg's invented "Chorale." As given in Floros, "Die Skizzen zum Violinkonzert," 122.

We know that Brahms was on Berg's mind when he was composing his concerto, for he said so to Louis Krasner in his letter of March 28, 1935: "From May onward I will compose 'our' violin concerto by the banks of the Wörthersee (diagonally across from Pörtschach where the violin concerto of Brahms was written)."[20] The omission of any specific mention of Brahms's Fourth Symphony here or elsewhere in Berg's extant correspondence signifies little. But if one accepts that the similarities between Berg's concerto and Brahms's symphony are, in sum, too many to be the result of pure chance, then it is natural that we should still ask what Berg might have wanted to express with them.

Schoenberg's statement in his lecture that Wagner and Brahms had "unif[ied] the thematic material" of their works in a "formalist manner" was naturally also intended to situate himself, and his method of composing with twelve tones, as their common heir at a time when he felt his legitimacy to be increasingly disputed by the antimodernists and anti-Semites

Example 3.3. "Es ist genug" as it appears in the cellos in mm. 158–61 in the second movement of Berg's Violin Concerto.

Example 3.4. The theme of Brahms's passacaglia in the last movement of his Fourth Symphony op. 98, mm. 1–8.

in Germany (his correspondence with Berg of late 1932 demonstrates clearly how much he was troubled by questions of "where I belong").[21] In the two years between Schoenberg's lecture and the composition of Berg's concerto, the former's pariah status had received further confirmation when he lost his teaching position in Berlin.

We can thus construct a narrative around Berg's Violin Concerto in which it is an affirmation of the Schoenberg school's claims to be the latter-day representatives of the Austro-German tradition and proof of its flourishing continuance. If Berg based his new work on a chain of thirds, then the connection to his (tonal) musical forefathers Brahms, Beethoven, Mozart, et al. would be obvious—he could hardly have done anything less secretive. His inclusion of a Bach chorale melody, to boot, with its harmonization alternating between Bach and Berg, was just added proof of his musical lineage. The final chord of the Violin Concerto—B♭ major with an added major sixth—also seems to refer directly to the close of Mahler's *Lied von der Erde*, yet another major work in the Austro-German canon that was of great importance to the Schoenberg school. By labeling the ländler a "Carinthian folk song" in the score and by adding the instruction "wienerisch" to certain passages, Berg further underlined his intention to place the work in a specifically Austro-Germanic, historical-geographical context. He was not the first of his "school" to quote from the Austro-German canon in a dodecaphonic work to emphasize his belonging to it—witness Webern's use of the B–A–C–H motive in the row for his String Quartet, or Schoenberg's use of the same motive in his Variations for Orchestra op. 31 (Taruskin writes aptly of its "screaming references to the musical cipher B–A–C–H proclaiming Germanic hegemony").[22] But the tonal context in which we hear the folk song and the chorale here make these references all the more insistent.

This interpretation of Berg's Violin Concerto as testimony to his own perceived place in history at a time of trial might ring true, but it still leaves

Manon Gropius out in the cold. And the one thing that all commentators have always agreed upon is that she was the real inspiration for the work. None of this is mutually exclusive—to be inspired by a tragic event is a *topos* in the history of western music that does not make invalid the possibility of other factors impinging upon the act of composition. But if Manon was supposedly so central to the work's conception, it can only be instructive to investigate Berg's relationship to her and her family.

Manon was born to Alma Mahler and her second husband, Walter Gropius, in 1916. She was and remained, by all accounts, Alma's favorite child. Alma seems to have considered Manon a perfect specimen of "Aryan" purity, whereas she regarded her other daughter, Anna Mahler, as racially "tainted" on account of her father's Jewish heritage. Alma's anti-Semitism is as incomprehensible today as it is undeniable. While Alma adored the Germanic manliness she saw in Gropius, their marriage became distinctly rocky when he had to go off on military duty. She began an affair with the writer Franz Werfel, despite her reservations about his Jewishness, and she soon bore a son, Martin, whom she was convinced was Werfel's child. He was born prematurely after a particularly vigorous night of sex with Werfel that left Alma lying in a pool of blood, and he died within just a few months.[23] Alma and Gropius divorced, she began living with Werfel, and finally married him in 1929. Werfel's increasing success as a writer allowed Alma to retain her position as one of the leading ladies of Viennese cultural circles. Her considerable influence was no secret. When in early 1933 Clemens Krauss learned that a newspaper interview he had given had incurred her displeasure, he immediately wrote her a letter of explanation that is little short of groveling—a remarkable document from a director of the Vienna State Opera more used to wielding power himself.[24]

Both Berg and his wife Helene knew Alma well. Helene had briefly helped to looked after Manon and Martin before the latter's death; Alma had financed the publication of the vocal score of *Wozzeck* in 1922 and received the dedication of the work; and the two couples—Alban and Helene, Alma and Franz—met many times over the years. Alma seems to have remained the dominant figure in her relationship with the Bergs, as was her wont in most of her friendships. Her correspondence with them is full of emotional bullying. Effusive declarations of affection alternate with accusations (sometimes implicit, sometimes explicit) that this affection is inadequately reciprocated. Dealing with Alma must have been exhausting. Small wonder that her relationship with Werfel was as turbulent as had been her relationships with former partners, nor can one blame him for having taken up rooms elsewhere for a while. Monogamy remained for

Alma a matter of intermittent interest, and in the early 1930s she began an affair with Johannes Hollnsteiner, a prominent Catholic priest who was both father-confessor to the Austrian politician Kurt Schuschnigg and a leading figure in relations between Vienna and the Vatican.

Germany's annexation of Austria in 1938 (the *Anschluss*) and the prominent place in the history books assigned to the Nazification of Austria and the fate of its Jews have largely obscured the fact that the regime supplanted by the Nazis was already fascist. "Austrofascism" had developed out of right-wing groupings formed after the First World War, primarily the Christian Social Party and the paramilitary "Heimwehr" (the "home guard," though wholly without the quaint connotations that the term has in English). Its adherents established a one-party state in Austria in early 1933 at roughly the same time that Hitler took power across the border. The Austrian chancellor, Engelbert Dollfuss, had been elected democratically in 1932, but now banned the Austrian socialist party and set up a dictatorship allied to Mussolini, whom he aimed to emulate as Austria's own "Duce" as well as he could. (This was not always easy, given that he was of particularly diminutive stature—his nickname was "Millimetternich.") The justice minister under Dollfuss was Kurt Schuschnigg. They were jointly responsible for the reintroduction of the death penalty, banned in Austria after the First World War, and they used it selectively, but unhesitatingly, against political enemies on the left. The emblem of the Austrofascists was the *Kruckenkreuz*, more obviously Christian in origin than the *Hakenkreuz*, and they cultivated a close relationship with the Catholic Church. Their aim was the creation of a "corporatist state" after the example of Mussolini's Italy, in which different groupings with specific vested interests, such as industry or the agricultural community, would be represented and consulted at the governmental level. Attempts to establish a singular Austrian identity were only partially successful, not least because powerful elements within Austria were keen to unite with Germany, their closest neighbor in matters of language and culture. A failed Nazi putsch in July 1934 resulted in the assassination of Dollfuss, following which Schuschnigg assumed office as Chancellor.

Alma Mahler's contacts with the Austrofascists were not confined to her affair with Schuschnigg's priest Hollnsteiner. She knew Schuschnigg and his cohorts well, including Anton Rintelen, the man who conspired with the Austrian Nazis in their putsch of 1934 and whom they had (briefly) declared Chancellor after Dollfuss's assassination. Alma's elder daughter Anna, a sculptress, began an affair with Schuschnigg after modeling a bust of him in the second half of 1934, and Franz Werfel apparently helped him on occasion with his speech-writing (Werfel's proximity to Schuschnigg also played a role in his being awarded the national order of merit, the "Österreichisches Verdienstkreuz für Wissenschaft und Kunst," first class, in 1937).[25] When Manon took ill with polio in Venice in April 1934, Schuschnigg personally arranged for her to be brought back to Vienna by train in what had formerly been the railway carriage of the Austrian Emperor. During her final year of life, when her health by turns improved and deteriorated, Manon became engaged to Erich Cyhlar, a young government functionary allied to Schuschnigg. The literature states that the engagement was Alma's doing alone, for the wheelchair-bound Manon was hardly able to get about town to meet young men. Since she reputedly "had no friends" at all,[26] it does seem possible that her role in her own engagement was a secondary one. When Manon died, Hollnsteiner gave the funeral oration and Schuschnigg himself was in the congregation (as was Berg; Alma was too upset to attend, and it was also her general custom to avoid funerals, even of those close to her). The speech that Hollnsteiner gave at Manon's grave extolled her virtues (see fig. 3.1): "She blossomed like a wonderful flower. She went through the world as pure as an angel. She was joy and love to many." But the funeral was also a macabre social event that had as much to do with the social status of Manon's parents as with the girl herself. Elias Canetti was there, as he was at the time in love with Anna Mahler. While he is not the most reliable of witnesses (he writes that Alma was present, whereas in fact she stayed away), he left a vivid, cynical account of the jostling that took place at the cemetery as upwardly-mobile attendees tried to be seen by the people who mattered.[27]

Hollnsteiner's words were echoed by Ludwig Karpath's obituary of Manon in the *Wiener Sonn- und Montags-Zeitung* of April 29, 1935, when he wrote that she "wandered like an angel among us."[28] The photos of Manon that are in the public domain show a pretty girl, one obviously doted on (in one photograph she is dressed up like the Infanta Margarita Teresa as painted by Velázquez), but hardly one whose physical features, as captured by the lens, would unerringly prompt the adjective "angelic." There are two other independent witnesses to her character, though neither has left us an opinion of any length. As Alma's sometime son-in-law, Ernst Krenek knew her family circumstances intimately but was as repelled as he was fascinated (Alma's style, he said, was "that of Wagner's Brünnhilde, transposed into the atmosphere of the *Fledermaus*).[29] Of Manon, he wrote in his memoirs that "much song and dance has been made about her. . . . I regret to say that I didn't like her at all, because it seemed to me that she was mistrustful and deceitful and played the role of decoy and spy for

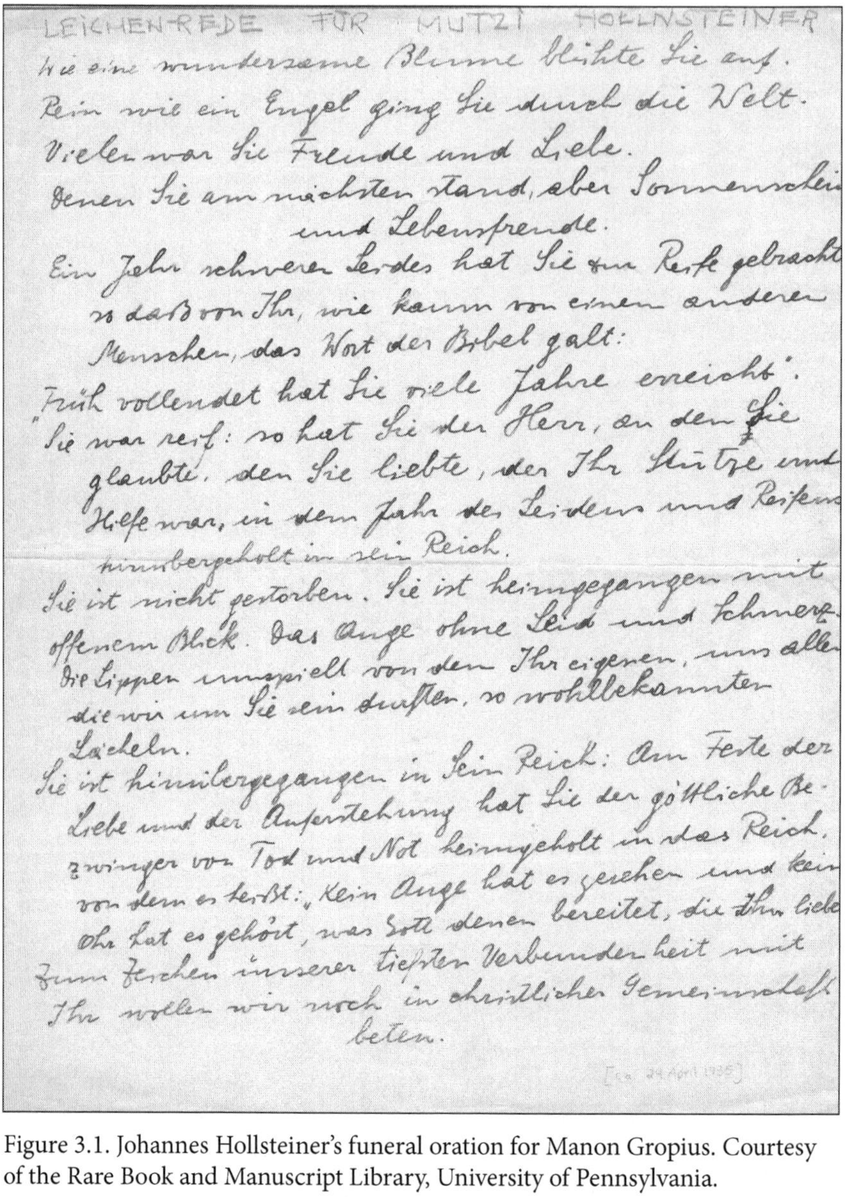

LEICHEN-REDE FÜR MUTZI HOLLNSTEINER

Wie eine wundersame Blume blühte Sie auf.
Rein wie ein Engel ging Sie durch die Welt.
Vielen war Sie Freude und Liebe.
Denen Sie am nächsten stand, aber Sonnenschein
und Lebensfreude.
Ein Jahr schweren Leides hat Sie zur Reife gebracht
so daß von Ihr, wie kaum von einem anderen
Menschen, das Wort der Bibel galt:
Früh vollendet hat Sie viele Jahre erreicht".
"Sie war reif: so hat Sie der Herr, an den Sie
glaubte, den Sie liebte, der Ihr Stütze und
Hilfe war, in dem Jahr des Leidens und Reifens
hinübergeholt in sein Reich.
Sie ist nicht gestorben. Sie ist heimgegangen mit
offenem Blick. Das Auge ohne Leid und Schmerz.
Die Lippen umspielt von dem Ihr eigenen, uns allen
die wir um Sie sein durften, so wohlbekannten
Lächeln.
Sie ist hinübergegangen in Sein Reich: Am Feste der
Liebe und der Auferstehung hat Sie der göttliche Be-
zwinger von Tod und Not heimgeholt in das Reich,
von dem es heißt: „Kein Auge hat es gesehen und kein
Ohr hat es gehört, was Gott denen bereitet, die Ihn lieben"
Zum Zeichen unserer tiefsten Verbundenheit mit
Ihr wollen wir noch in christlicher Gemeinschaft
beten.

[ca. 24 April 1935]

Figure 3.1. Johannes Hollsteiner's funeral oration for Manon Gropius. Courtesy of the Rare Book and Manuscript Library, University of Pennsylvania.

her mother. May God forgive me if I'm wrong about her."[30] And Manon's piano teacher Hans Erich Apostel recalled in later years that she had been a "spoiled brat."[31] We are hardly going to know for sure now, but it is likely that the truth about her lay somewhere in between: that she was a moderately pretty girl who could be angelic sometimes and, at others, a deceitful brat. In short, a teenage girl much like any other. It is not surprising, however, that Alma should after her death have idealized her, casting her as a paragon of physical and spiritual beauty.

For the distraught Alma, others could not mourn enough. In her correspondence with the Bergs immediately after Manon's death, she expressed her grief in forms of emotional bullying far more intense than any she had before employed with them. Alma had instructed her servant to let no one see her while she was in mourning, and this allowed her to complain that her friends had cast her off. In numerous undated letters in the days and weeks after Manon's death, she wrote to the Bergs variously, "My beloved ones, why have you abandoned me at *this* time! I so expected and needed you"; "in all my misery I missed you both—the ones nearest to me—so much. . . . Why did you not just *come* on the strength of our love?"; "I still cannot comprehend that you let yourselves be shooed away from being near me by clumsy, new servants"; "why don't you write to me. . . . I always felt that your modesty—which isn't modesty—would at some time do something dreadful to us. At this most terrible time in my life you left me alone"; and "it is awful that I did not have you at that time—*how* I needed *you, just you.*"[32]

To judge from her correspondence in general, hyperbole had long been Alma's favored mode of discourse. We have already noted the effusive nature of her letters to the Bergs, in which even the usual opening terms of address are insufficiently expressive and are replaced by "Meine Geliebten" (my beloved ones) or the superlative, "Meine Geliebtesten" (my most beloved ones). A prime example of Alma's pompous epistolary rhetoric is to be found in a love letter written during the First World War to her then husband Gropius. Even given the conventions of the times, Alma's pseudopoetics are absurdly grandiloquent when she writes of how she longs for him to return so that she might kneel and let him place his "holy member in my mouth."[33] Nothing, it seems, could in Alma's radius be everyday or commonplace. Even a blow job had to be a religious experience.

The dynamic of the correspondence between Alma and the Bergs after Manon's death makes Berg's promise of a dedication well-nigh inevitable. It was probably the only way that Berg could prove his loyalty at a time of distress and stop her haranguing him. It is almost as if Alma expected it of him. But Berg's letter announcing the dedication of his latest work "to the memory of an angel," quoted at the outset here, is notable because of the manner in which the dedication is set off from the body of the text. It is treated as if it were a quotation—in other words, something for whose veracity he is unwilling to vouch himself. And a "quotation" is what it is, for the description of Manon as an "angel" had, it seems, already become the only acceptable form of reference to her among the immediate circle of family and friends—witness the graveside words of Hollnsteiner and Karpath's obituary. Alma's insistence on Manon's perfection would allow for no other description. It was undoubtedly intended to imply that she had been "too good for the world" (a notion also expressed in the Bergs' letters to Alma). Bruno Walter in his memoirs calls her "angelic" twice in the space of a paragraph,[34] while the chapter in Canetti's memoirs about Manon's death is entitled "Burial of an Angel" (though his intent was presumably ironic).[35] It even seems to have been transferred to others in Alma's immediate circle if a correspondent of hers found it advisable—thus in a letter to her, Bruno Walter once even referred to Hollnsteiner's own "angelicness."[36] If Berg were to dedicate a work to the memory of Manon, it could only be to her as "angel," for by now any other description would have been tantamount to an affront in Alma's eyes.

Why would Berg have been so keen to appease Alma? The most obvious answer is that he always had been. This had been the dynamic of their relationship since Berg had been a composing unknown and she the widow of his idol, Gustav Mahler. He was in her debt too—not only had she financed the publication of the *Wozzeck* vocal score, but she had provided money toward his purchase of a car in 1930. Given the poor state of his finances in 1935, he must have known he might need to call on her again.[37] She was also one of the go-betweens for Berg and his lover Hanna Fuchs (her sister-in-law, as mentioned above), and such knowledge gives one power (Alma was still fulfilling this function as late as December 1934). Helene Berg ostensibly knew nothing of Hanna, and Alma had hitherto supposedly remained silent on the matter, despite her relationship with Helene being more intimate than her friendship with Alban. Berg was in fact just one figure in a convoluted network of relationships that had Alma at its epicenter.

Let us sum this up: Alma is married to Werfel; Berg has an affair with Werfel's sister (thus Alma's sister-in-law); Werfel helps write speeches for the Austrian Chancellor Schuschnigg, whose father confessor Hollnsteiner is Alma's lover; Schuschnigg is the lover of Alma's first daughter Anna, whose second husband (Ernst Krenek) has written an opera with Alma's former lover Kokoschka and whose third husband (Paul Zsolnay) is the publisher of her father's letters and her stepfather's novels; and Alma's second daughter is engaged to a member of Schuschnigg's political entourage. To describe this circle as socially incestuous is an understatement, and their sexual roundabout brings to mind fin-de-siècle plays such as Arthur Schnitzler's *Reigen* or (more pertinently here) Wedekind's two *Lulu* plays, *Erdgeist* and *Büchse der Pandora*, which feature precisely such convoluted networks of sexual and familial relations.

We cannot exclude the possibility that Berg found the *Lulu* topic attractive precisely because it mirrored the social and artistic stratum in which he lived and worked. Perhaps he even saw it as a chance to parody Alma herself, as a kind of silent declaration of independence from her overbearing friendship. But by the early 1930s, the cultural climate was no longer conducive to a *Lulu*. Berg might have been Viennese, the play itself from the fin de siècle, but his opera was clearly a child of the Weimar era and its garish approach to life and art—the era of the Brecht/Weill *Seven Deadly Sins, Mahagonny*, and *Dreigroschenoper*; of *Jonny spielt auf*; of Sally Bowles and *Goodbyes to Berlin*. *Lulu* was not what mealy-mouthed Catholic Austrofascists would have found uplifting at a time of nationalist resurgence. But Berg needed it to make him money. His *Lulu Suite*, performed by Erich Kleiber in Berlin in December 1934, had been a public relations disaster. Kleiber resigned his position within a week, and the prospects of Berg's music receiving any further performances in Germany diminished to nothing. That meant a massive drop in royalties at a time when half of the Berg's household budget was being spent on medicines.[38] He was also helping his sister Smaragda with money, and the mental instability of Helene's brother Franz put a further financial burden on them. America offered new possibilities, and Berg was able to raise money by selling the score of *Wozzeck* to the Library of Congress. He even tried to sell the score of the *Lyric Suite* in England via Adorno. The $1,500 promised by Krasner for a violin concerto was money that could be made within just a few months and was thus immensely tempting. But as *Wozzeck* had proven, opera was the way to make real money in the music world, and Berg was banking on *Lulu* to generate similar funds in order to finance his later middle age. In a letter to Adorno of February 19, 1935, in which he discussed his money problems, he wrote that "when other times come (and they *will* come) and *Lulu* is performed on stage, everything will be well again."[39]

Berg would have known that the best way to win the favor of the authorities in advance of any prospective Austrian première of *Lulu* was to get political support right at the top. Thanks to Alma, Berg had enjoyed contact with the leading Austrofascists since shortly after they took power in early 1933. His letter of April 12, 1933, to his wife mentions a meeting about editions of music for schools at the offices of his publisher Universal Edition together with "Almschi—[and] Rintelen" (Anton Rintelen being at the time the Minister of Education).[40] Three weeks later, he wrote to her that he had visited Paul Zsolnay and was about to leave when Schuschnigg came; so he stayed, and "we politicized for an hour still, and we also spoke a lot about music, all quite naturally and intimately."[41] A week after that, on May 15, he wrote that Alma had arranged for him to attend a dinner on the following Thursday "with Rintelen, Furtwängler, Schuschnigg, General Wagner, Perntner,"[42] and on May 18 he wrote to her of the "Brahms-Fest" to which he had been invited the day before, where the Austrian President Wilhelm Miklas and Chancellor Dollfuss were present, and where both Schuschnigg and Furtwängler gave speeches on the composer (though Furtwängler's speech annoyed him because of its "Nazi leanings" and because of Furtwängler's insistence that Brahms was the "last representative of German music." "The Schoenberg circle was not even mentioned as existing," complained Berg.[43] Rintelen was dismissed as Education Minister on May 24, much to Alma's displeasure, though she remained in close contact with him. On August 7, 1933, Alma wrote to the Bergs that "the Schuschniggs want to see you. We spoke of that!" though we do not know if anything concrete came of it.

By early 1935 Berg must have realized that his *Lulu* would not soon see the light of day in Nazi Germany, so support at home was all the more important. Schuschnigg, having meanwhile acceded to the Chancellorship, was obviously the one who could smooth over any difficulties, and the easiest way to him was still through Alma. He could also be accessed via Hollnsteiner (the filmmaker Rudolf Forster and the conductor Hermann Scherchen later chose this path with success).[44] So the best way for Berg to ingratiate himself with them all was surely to dedicate an accessible work "to the memory of an angel," the same angel whom Schuschnigg had ferried back to Vienna in the imperial railway carriage and whom Hollnsteiner had celebrated in his graveside valediction. Berg's relationship with Schuschnigg was close enough for him to write a personal letter of condolence when Schuschnigg's wife was killed in a car accident in July 1935. In it, he offered "words of comfort," quoting the text to the Bach chorale he was employing in his Violin Concerto, stating specifically that he had "just that minute" written the last bars of an orchestral arrangement of it when he heard the "terrible news" of the accident on the radio[45] (it is perhaps reading too much between the lines here, but it is difficult to avoid the impression that, had he not already promised Alma a concerto in memory of her angel, he might for expediency's sake have dedicated it to the memory of Schuschnigg's "angel" instead). Three months later, on October 15, 1935, Berg contributed ten schillings to a Christmas charity sponsored by Schuschnigg and in his accompanying letter told the Chancellor frankly of the financial difficulties arising from the attitudes taken toward his music both in the Third Reich and in "the New Austria." He may have hoped that Schuschnigg would order a change in official policy, but in any case, it was too late, for Berg was already ill and would die within ten weeks.[46]

Berg might have been actively pursuing the support of the Schuschnigg party, but his connections were not solely to the upper echelons of Austrian fascism. His pupil and confidante Willi Reich was the official translator for the complete edition of Mussolini's writings, being issued in German by the Zurich publisher Rascher in the mid-1930s. This was no galley work done for money, but a labor of love, as Reich proudly wrote in an article entitled "A Viennese Musician Translates Mussolini" published in *Anbruch* in April/May 1935.[47] He had come across Mussolini's article "La dottrina del fascismo" while doing music research in Bologna in 1933 and had responded immediately: "This is what I've long been searching for!" Reich was bewitched by the "musicality" of the prose and its "rousing gestures" and promptly translated the article for his own pleasure. The experience— "in constant contact with the intellectual aura of the Duce"—gripped him so "passionately" that he claimed to have worked on it for "a day and two nights almost without interruption" (ironically, the article had actually been ghostwritten for Mussolini by Giovanni Gentile). Reich had sent his translation to Mussolini's office; they sent it to Rascher, who then in turn asked Reich to undertake a complete translation of the Duce's writings. Reich's contribution to the edition went beyond mere translation, for he also on occasion added extensive commentary, as in his essay on Mussolini's notion of the "corporatist state"—a topic that Reich might have chosen because it was one that preoccupied the leaders of his own country.[48] On March 18, 1938, just a few days after the *Anschluss*, Reich's publisher (situated in neutral Switzerland) wrote to say it had become widely known that he was Jewish. This meant that sales would be almost impossible in greater Germany, the publisher's biggest market, and so they respectfully declined his further services as translator, effective immediately.[49] It is noteworthy that Reich had already gone into exile in Switzerland a full month before the *Anschluss*; perhaps his political connections had warned him in advance of the inevitable, or perhaps he had simply read all the signs that so many others ignored.

One must not imagine that Berg's friends were all fascist sympathizers, for he also remained close to Theodor Adorno, who was both allied to
the left and himself of Jewish extraction (though he in turn had no compunction in collaborating with Reich both on the music journal *23* and on
the latter's study of Berg published after the composer's death). Berg's am-
bivalent, longtime emotional connection to Schoenberg, a Jew, remained
largely unaltered by political events, and his declarations of undying love
to Hanna Fuchs, another Jew, continued. We should remember that during Berg's final years political alliances were not as solidified as one might
imagine in hindsight. The number of men and women in Germany and
Austria who saw clearly the lay of the land in 1933 after Hitler's accession to power and took appropriate steps to remove themselves—as did
Schoenberg—was relatively small. The majority assumed that some form
of rational normality must soon establish itself—hence the efforts on the
part of many, ranging from Adorno to Hindemith and Berg, to accommo-
date themselves to the political situation. We must resist the temptation to
equate Italian and Austrian fascism of this time directly with the Nazism of
their rabid cousin to the north. Mussolini's alliance with Hitler and impo-
sition of a state-sanctioned anti-Semitism analog to the Nuremberg Laws
still lay in the future. As Richard Taruskin has observed, "Mussolini's Italy,
until the Ethiopian adventure anyway, behaved more like one of those cozy
authoritarian regimes neoconservatives like Jeanne Kirkpatrick used to
tout in the waning days of the cold war, keeping the trains on schedule,
and offering cooperative artists a bottomless feeding trough."[50] Mussolini
only began his colonial war in Ethiopia in October 1935, and for any thinking person it should have erased all doubts as to the potential brutality of
his regime.

The Austrofascist state was in many respects little different from the
Italian one, having seen as yet neither large-scale purges nor concentration
camps after the Nazi model. Yet it is an inescapable fact that Austria under
Dollfuss and Schuschnigg was a one-party, fascist dictatorship that employed violence against its opponents, set up internment camps to house
them (the number of political detainees reached five figures within a year
of the abolition of democracy), and in several cases used the legal system to
ensure that the most troublesome of them met their deaths. And it is equal-
ly undeniable that Berg gave Austrofascism his wholehearted support. Nor
did he hesitate to curry favor across the border. He protested vigorously
when he was classified as "Jewish" in Germany and wrote to the authorities
to affirm his Aryan lineage[51] (after Adorno had urged him to do so);[52] he
wrote to Reich on April 28, 1934, to suggest that in his writings he should

emphasize Richard Strauss's Jewish connections in order to cast aspersions on Strauss's "Aryan" status in Nazi Germany;[53] then there is the unpleasant caricature of a Jewish banker in *Lulu*. This has often been excused as an aberration, though it is just one more example of Berg's willingness to indulge in compromise. It was the official reason given for Schoenberg's refusal to complete *Lulu* after his friend's death,[54] though since Schoenberg had already suspected Berg of overdue lenience toward the Nazis, he presumably saw it within a greater context of political unsoundness; and as Antony Beaumont has suggested, while Berg's characterization of Lulu and the Painter might have been modeled on Alma and Kokoschka, Schoenberg would surely have understood them as referring to his first wife's affair with the painter Richard Gerstl, who had committed suicide in 1908 when Mathilde Schoenberg decided to stay with her husband.[55] When Hindemith, not yet himself non grata, had dangled before Berg the possibility of a teaching post at the Hochschule für Musik in Berlin in May 1933, Berg's report of it to his wife showed him less disinclined to accept than one might imagine, given that Schoenberg was in the process of losing his job at the Akademie in the same city—indeed, Berg seemed somewhat attracted by the fact that his former teacher was about to be ousted:

> Even if we don't consider accepting such a proposal (although now, as Schoenberg may not be in Berlin any more, it would be more open for discussion than it would have been earlier), it would be a colossal triumph for me to be engaged by the Nazis (think above all of Eberstaller and of Almschi) and something we could play off against the Viennese government if they really come with an offer, or if they hesitate because I'm not right-wing enough for them.[56]

Apart from Berg's joy at the prospect of impressing Richard Eberstaller, Alma's brother-in-law and a prominent Nazi sympathizer, what astonishes most about this letter is Berg's coldness toward the imminent sacking of Schoenberg. Berg knew of his teacher's envy at the financial success of *Wozzeck*, and his continuing psychological dependence on Schoenberg was colored by unspoken resentments on both sides. Yet his commitment to the Schoenbergian cause was undimmed, just as his awareness of his debt to the man remained undisputed. So Berg's nonchalant mention of Schoenberg's loss of livelihood—at the age of nearly sixty, just after starting a new family with his second wife—seems cold-hearted to the point of cruelty.

Then there is the matter of Berg's early plan to base his concerto on the motto of the Gymnastics Association: "frisch, fromm, fröhlich, frei." In

Austria, this *Turnerbund* had been widely infiltrated by Nazi sympathizers (the Nazi Party, being banned at the time, had chosen it as one of several suitable platforms for its underground activities). Several of the Nazi plotters for the coup of July 1934 were members of the Association, and their final meeting point before the attempted putsch was their "Turnerhalle" (gymnastics hall) on the Siebensterngasse, just a mile away from the Chancellor's office. If Berg had wanted to make a statement in support of the right-wing nationalist forces in Austria, then incorporating the *Turnerbund*'s motto would have been a suitable first step, as it was a widely known phrase that did not display any open commitment to National Socialism, yet was still clear in its far-right implications. Douglas Jarman has observed that Berg's sketches reverse the order of the four words (to "frei, fröhlich, fromm, frisch") and proposes that this is an implicit "rejection . . . of the nationalism inherent in the motto."[57] However, if Berg had wanted to take a private, hidden stand against nationalism, then he could have incorporated any number of anti-Nazi slogans in a manner so that no one else would have needed to know, instead of rotating a nationalist slogan. There appears to be nothing of that kind among his sketches. We must in all fairness consider that Berg's interest in the motto could also have been prompted by the *Turnerkreuz*, the "gymnast's cross" emblem that used the association's motto in graphic form, arranging the four *F*'s in a square. Its form, with twelve outer "points," contains numerous symmetries that would have appealed to Berg (and suggests that the order of the four *F*'s is in fact interchangeable; see fig. 3.2).

But however much these geometrical matters might have intrigued Berg, the political implications of the *Turnerbund* would have remained unaltered, and to use its motto might have implied to Schuschnigg's party that the composer hoped another putsch against them might be more successful than the last. Berg's early sketches for the Violin Concerto either preceded or coincided with the trial of Rintelen, the conspirators' would-be chancellor, which began on March 3, 1935, and ended a fortnight later with a verdict of life imprisonment. Perhaps Berg was at the time pondering which faction might be better appeased and now decided against the pro-Germans in favor of the Austrofascists, who were determined to maintain a separate national identity. This might explain why he abandoned any hint of "frisch, fromm, fröhlich, frei" and instead placed a focus on local color in his Concerto. In an anonymous article in *Anbruch* not long after his death, the use of the Carinthian folk song in particular was indeed interpreted as an endeavor to write a work that was specifically "Austrian."[58] Since Willi Reich was the journal's main source of information on his

Figure 3.2. The *Turnerkreuz* with its four *F*'s.

friend, this might well have been Berg's own intention (*Anbruch* at this time reflected the Schuschnigg government's stance by being insistently Austrian in its choice of article topics).

Berg's attempted rapprochement with the ascendant right-wing powers in both Germany and Austria was probably a result of opportunism rather than of conviction. While the published letters and reminiscences of his family, friends, and colleagues offer little proof of *active* support for fascism (except for his obvious attempts to endear himself to Schuschnigg), neither do they contain any hint of active opposition to it. The only picture they paint is one of acquiescence and tentative appeasement. When Berg complained to Adorno just six weeks before his death that he was "too little Catholic for the Catholics and too little Jewish for the Jews" in order to get ahead on the Austrian music scene,[59] it was less a spur-of-the-moment quip than a confirmation that he was trying to appear differently to different people in order to survive and succeed. Politics were for Berg a movable feast.

All this suggests a degree of calculation on the part of Berg that stands in contradiction to the generous portrait of the man found in much of the literature. But when it comes to Berg's compositions, "calculating" was evidently an important part of his art. Research into Berg's work in the past thirty years has revealed assorted "secret programs" bound up with a complex numerological symbolism. Berg himself wrote an "open letter" to Schoenberg in 1925 in which he revealed the main numerological and personal references in the Chamber Concerto that he had just dedicated to Schoenberg on his fiftieth birthday. He even intimated that there was much more still to find, teasing his readers that adherents of program music would rejoice if they could find all the other personal references he had built into the work. It has been argued cogently by Brenda Dalen and others that these references extend to a critical description of Schoenberg's turbulent relationship with his wife Mathilde, who had died in 1923 after a marriage punctuated by adultery, abandonment, rapprochement, and estrangement.[60] Derrick Puffett was one of the few commentators to suggest a darker side to Berg on the basis of this new musical-cum-biographical evidence. Writing of Berg's supposed depiction of Schoenberg's first marriage in the Chamber Concerto, Puffett asks:

> Isn't it extraordinary that Berg should put all this "red-hot" material, these details of Schoenberg's private life . . . into a work supposedly meant as a homage for him?
>
> One is tempted to call it "Berg's revenge." Somewhere in his mind there must have been a demon, angry and bitter after all the slights, all the taken-for-granteds, all the carefully timed withholdings of praise, who longed to tell the world about his teacher's personal failure. . . . And Berg's decision to "tell the world about it" in his Chamber Concerto, *even if nobody in the world was ever supposed to know* . . . has something of the same calculated cruelty that one observes in his portrait of Wozzeck.[61]

Berg's next major work, the *Lyric Suite*, used similar means to document infidelities, only this time they were his own. It was prompted by his first meeting with Hanna Fuchs, with whose family Berg stayed in Prague in mid-May 1925 when he visited the city to attend a performance of his *Three Fragments from "Wozzeck."* Hanna (née Werfel, Franz's sister) was married to the industrialist Herbert Fuchs, with whom she had two children. Berg became immediately infatuated. Over the next ten years he wrote her a series of passionate love letters and encoded their names and initials in his works, beginning with the *Lyric Suite*. He also based many of his compositional structures on a number symbolism in which he assigned the number 23 to himself and the number 10 to Hanna. As Jarman has observed, he seems to have based his symbolism in part on the writings of Wilhelm Fliess, an erstwhile colleague of Freud's who favored nasal surgery to solve psychosexual conditions and also developed odd theories about "periodic numbers" that supposedly determine human existence. Twenty-three was for him the "male number," 28 the "female" (for obvious reasons if reckoned in days). The latter number also acquires structural significance in Berg's works.[62] Apart from the brief song "Schliesse mir die Augen beide," the *Lyric Suite* was Berg's first proper foray into dodecaphony. Since his adoption of the twelve-note system coincides with an increasing interest in using numbers to determine the structures of his music, it would seem that, far from constricting Berg (and despite his initial claim that working with the method proceeded slowly),[63] Schoenberg's system provided him serendipitously with just the tools that he needed to set his number-bound imagination free.

In a letter of April 16, 1936, to Helene Berg, nearly four months after Alban's death, Theodor Adorno wrote to reassure her that "The matter of H. F. was *not* of central importance to him . . . he loved H. F. far more in order to be able to write the Lyric Suite, than that he wrote the Lyric Suite for love." Hanna, he wrote snobbishly, was "a romantic mistake—she is bourgeois through and through." (Despite his avowed left-wing sympathies, Adorno long retained a deep attraction to the old order and here implicitly acknowledges Helene's higher status as a presumed illegitimate daughter of Emperor Franz Josef.)[64] We do not know when Helene found out about Hanna Fuchs, though Adorno's openness about the affair so soon after Alban's death suggests that it was not a recent shock. Helene herself referred snidely to "the well-off people from Prague" in a letter to Alma of May 1936,[65] yet felt above-it-all enough to offer Hanna Fuchs the manuscript of the *Lyric Suite* on permanent loan shortly afterward. We cannot know how Helene really felt, but this does not seem the action of a woman who has suddenly discovered a decade-long infidelity on the part of her deceased husband. In one of his first letters to Hanna, Berg mentions that his behavior upon returning from Prague had prompted Alma Mahler into guessing almost immediately the truth about his new passion (she would soon be smuggling his letters to Hanna on her occasional trips to Prague). Berg adds that "my wife also noticed something" and had asked if he was "still in Prague" in his mind. He assures Hanna that his wife does not suspect the real truth, though upon reading his letter, one cannot help but see this as wishful thinking. Berg here also implies that Helene had put an end to their sex life some time before (thus when he was not yet out of his thirties), writing of "her illness that now has lain for months, almost years between us."[66] If our interpretation is correct, perhaps Helene was not even surprised when she learnt that her husband had sought physical release elsewhere. After all, if one is the illegitimate daughter of the Emperor and one's friends number serial adulterers such as Alma Mahler, then one cannot claim that extramarital sex is either unknown or unacceptable in one's social class. But when Adorno consoled Helene after Berg's death that his relationship with Hanna had been of no higher significance, what he seems to mean is that it was "just" about sex. And if he truly thought that Helene would regard an exchange of bodily fluids as a trivial matter, it speaks volumes about Adorno's own cavalier attitude toward her gender. This notion of her higher, "spiritual" bond with Alban was indeed one that Helene did need and propagate, though it surely resulted from her desperation to reassure herself that she had remained somehow special, regardless of whose orifices might have enveloped her husband's procreative organ. The "higher" she regarded their union, the more one suspects that she was deeply hurt by her husband's delight in everything lower.

Yet it is by no means certain that Berg's relationship with Hanna ever got that far. He rarely met her, and the high point of their relationship, to judge from his own words, was "the holiest—the very, very great eternal moments in the library" that took place at the beginning of their relationship.[67] While we cannot rule out the possibility that Hanna was happy to have a quickie with her back against a bookshelf from a man she barely knew, it would hardly have been the kind of excitingly romantic encounter likely to furnish her with fantasies for months to come. It seems more likely that nothing really happened at all, with Berg's insistent adverbs and adjectives a kind of ersatz for the deed itself. Altogether, Berg's letters to Hanna have an unreal, staged quality about them and reveal strange obsessions. In the letter to Hanna quoted above, Berg wrote of the "crazily intoxicating sight of the sultry, sweet secrets of your armpits."[68] What on earth might Hanna have made of this, apparently the first lengthy letter she received from him? She must have been perplexed that a man so enamored of her should fantasize openly about her sweaty armpit hair. The illogicality of Berg's non sequiturs ("sweet" is a taste, not a sight; and if something is sighted, then it is not a secret) suggests that his fantasies were the result of his failure to reach any other "sultry secrets" of her anatomy, sweet or otherwise.

Berg's letters to Hanna also show him to be strangely uninventive, laden as they are with cumbersome similes and metaphors. In a letter of November 16, 1926, he writes of how she has developed "like the noblest wines in your husband's [wine] cellar." Even if one accepts that Berg's generation might not have found this as sexist as we do today, one still cannot help wondering why this man, who created worlds in sound of such astonishing originality, could think of nothing better to write to the supposed love of his life. His letters suggest that Hanna remained for him an ideal, someone existing only on an imaginary pedestal. And such an attitude is usually possible only if the man thus impassioned has not come close enough to experience the object of his passion as a real human being. To turn Berg's own example around: the closer one's acquaintance with sweaty armpits, the less sweet and secret they usually seem.

Quotation is also another habit of Berg's in his correspondence. Thus Hanna is his "immortal beloved" in his letter of July 23, 1925, and in his letter of November 16, 1926, he even descends into near-plagiarism. In this letter, which Berg declares at the outset to be an *Abschiedsbrief* (farewell letter), he bemoans the impossibility of a *Vereinigung* (union) with Hanna, with this word repeated three times in rapid succession. It reads like a parody of Wagner's farewell letter to Mathilde Wesendonck of July 6, 1858, in which he also insisted on the impossibility of their *Vereinigung* while trying to prompt her into admitting the possibility of it.[69] The Wagner-Wesendonck letters, the most famous correspondence between any composer and his muse, would have been known to Berg for years. The aura of renunciation in this *Abschiedsbrief*, plus the references to *Tristan* in Berg's other correspondence of this autumn—in his letter to Hanna of October 23, 1926, he had even "deciphered" the opening of that opera as an encoded reference to their initials—suggest that Berg wanted to see his relationship with Hanna as a latter-day equivalent to that of Wagner and Mathilde Wesendonck.[70]

No letters from Hanna to Berg survive. While one could imagine Helene having destroyed any love letters she might have found after Berg's death, it seems that Hanna never actually wrote him any. She did, however, correspond occasionally with Helene, and Berg admits in his letters to Hanna that these were his only source of news of her. Reading his one-sided correspondence is rather depressing and uncomfortably voyeuristic. Poor Berg seems completely intoxicated with the woman, but in return has to make do with letters from her to his wife. This affair with Hanna (inasmuch as it ever was an "affair") has become stylized in the literature as the greatest passion of Berg's life, not least because their combined initials and "their" numbers determine so much of his music during the ten years between their first acquaintance and his death. But if the affair indeed took place mostly in his head, then perhaps Adorno was right, and the fantasy provided Berg with a more powerful emotional experience than he might have enjoyed had their relationship become less imagined and more real. And as Berg well knew, Wagner had completed *Tristan* far away from the woman who had inspired it.

Since George Perle first made known the existence of a "secret program" for the *Lyric Suite* that centered on Berg's relationship with Hanna,[71] various articles and books have claimed to discover new "secrets" in Berg's music above and beyond his obsession with her, positing new numbers of significance and offering new conundrums regarding works that seem to contain secrets that resist being teased out.[72] We should perhaps see this phenomenon in Bergian scholarship as part of a general trend, for the revelation of his "secret numbers" took place in the same decade as the publication in English of Ernö Lendvai's Fibonacci analyses of Bartók's works and an increasing interest in Bach's numerology. These studies were followed in the early 1980s by Roy Howat's *Debussy in Proportion*, in which that composer's structural use of the Golden Section was examined.[73] Perhaps the hunt for "meanings" in Berg was bound up, too, with the death throes of modernism, which was under attack from the neoromantics and postmodernists. Musicologists were now all the more eager to prove that the atonal music generated by a twelve-note row is far from arbitrary, and that constructivist composition can convey love and heartbreak as well as any music before it.[74]

If one is convinced of the existence of things hidden, then it is likely that one will find them, whether or not they are really there. As the hunt for secret meanings in Berg and elsewhere has proven, the more obscure and unlikely they seem, the better they can be believed: after all, they are supposed to be secret and thus well hidden. Overinterpretation of a work's program is tempting. For example, if the "Miazzl" mentioned in that Carinthian folk song in the Violin Concerto does indeed refer to Berg's early lover Marie Scheuchl, one could even argue that he chose it as a pun on her name—a "Vogelscheuch" being the German for "scarecrow" (literally a "bird scarer"), in possible reference to the scare her pregnancy had given him after his little bird had twittered in her plum tree. If one further considers that Hanna Fuchs had a sister called "Mizzi," another form of "Miazzl," things risk getting even more absurdly complicated. But the truth might be simpler: what if Berg just liked the tune and found its text delightfully vulgar, with the actual name in it quite irrelevant? Berg's pleasure in smut is demonstrated by a surviving doodle that he made on the back of a letter received from Webern's pupil Carl Buchman (dated September 17, 1933), featuring a sketch of male genitalia (seemingly rigid but neither particularly erect nor elongated) and also of a naked, squatting woman squirting gaseous substances and the letters *AL* from her alimentary canal while apparently planting a shrubbery. The letters *AL* are also drawn on the scrotum of the aforementioned genitalia and on other items featured on the same sketch, such as a shamrock (?), turnips, spider's webs, and what could either be a teacup or even (given the context) a chamber pot.[75] The female figure's breasts have been enlarged as an afterthought. Since the letters B[A?]N also appear on the sheet, AL could refer to Berg's first name, though we do not know what EL, IM, LE, or IG could mean. Another possibility would be AL[ma], with whom the Bergs were engaged in a difficult correspondence in late September and early October 1933. She was in the midst of her affair with Hollnsteiner, was showing a particular antipathy toward all things Jewish, and now found herself (or perhaps placed herself) at the focal point of her circle's reaction to Schoenberg's reconversion to Judaism. She coordinated both the dissemination of an explanatory letter from Schoenberg and Werfel's reply to him.[76] If AL signifies her, it could explain why the letters are at the center of a spider's web; and since the farting woman is not untypical for traditional depictions of witches (who, along with the devil, were long associated with leaving behind them noxious, sulfurous odors), she could also refer to Alma (the shrubbery might in that case even be a broomstick). Whatever their precise import, these drawings are what one might expect to see scribbled by a thirteen-year-old boy on the back of a school toilet door, not by a grown man in his late forties on the back of a letter. Numerous other rough sketches and cartoons by Berg have survived on the backs of letters and occasional documents. Sometimes he drew his own face, sometimes the faces of others, sometimes musical instruments, birds, or his house in the countryside. A few sketches are of female nudes in semilascivious poses. On at least two occasions, he made such sketches in connection with Alma Mahler. One is on the back of the draft of a letter to her dated July 11, 1923, and features three female nudes, one of whom is wearing high heels and holds, in her left hand, a large, upside-down head, à la Salome. It is impossible to tell if these sketches depict any specific woman.[77] Another such sketch was kept in an envelope on which Helene Berg at some point wrote "Drawing A.[lma] M.[ahler] a[nd] A.[lban] B.[erg] when he was on military duty." It depicts a naked woman with long flowing hair down to her heels, heavily pregnant, with a distended navel, prominent nipples and hairy pudenda striding with open legs toward a man in soldier's uniform with a dagger at his belt, who is holding toward her what is either the hilt of a knobbly-ended sword or a highly elongated, erect, black penis.[78] What the relation between the drawing and Alma Mahler could be remains a mystery (the only obvious connection is that Alma was pregnant with Manon while Berg was in the army). Apart from the first sketch mentioned above, no other Bergian doo-doo doodles seem to have survived,[79] though perhaps any others he made were consigned by Helene to a bonfire of the vulgarities.

Figure 3.3. The reverse of Berg's letter to Carl Buchman of September 17, 1933. Reproduced with permission from Musiksammlung, Österreichische Nationalbibliothek.

The hunt for the hidden in Berg has ironically obscured the fact, arguably more remarkable, that he was quite candid about his supposed secrets. He wrote no open letter about the *Lyric Suite* as he had about the Chamber Concerto—that would have been tactless. But from his letters to Hanna Fuchs and comments made by Helene, Adorno, and Reich, it is evident that everyone around him was aware of Berg's obsession with the numbers 10 and 23. When Willi Reich founded a new music journal in 1932, Berg got him to give it the title "23." If one has a secret and wants to keep it, then it seems odd to name a journal after it (though the editors admittedly did claim that it was officially named after paragraph 23 of the Austrian press laws). Berg furthermore annotated a score of the *Lyric Suite* to give to Hanna in which he laid everything bare. Had he wished all these matters to remain secret to the world then he could have told her in person, or just telephoned her when her husband was out. Committing his secrets to paper, doing so in such an elaborate form and in the near-certainty, furthermore, that Hanna would keep these precious documents safe, is a sign that they were in fact destined for posterity. All in all, one could almost assert that there has rarely been a composer so constructivist who was also less secretive about it.

Berg might have told Hanna Fuchs repeatedly of his undiminished passion for her in the decade between their first meeting and his death, but her status was by no means unique, for he was a serial philanderer. In November 1932 Berg wrote to Hanna, assuring her that his feelings for her remained as on their first day together and hoping beyond hope to see her again.[80] But just a month later, on December 17, 1932, he wrote to another lover, the actress Edith Edwards, whom he had met half a year before, assuring her in turn that his feelings for her had also remained unchanged and hoping beyond hope to see her again.[81] He was at this time also continuing a long-distance affair with Anny Askenase, wife of the pianist Stefan. A letter from Berg to Anny of late March 1933 describes the subterfuge with which he is trying to organize a meeting between them while his wife is away in April, and giving precise instructions as to how they must act if Helene invites Anny to tea during the latter's forthcoming stay in Vienna: "We have to speak very nonchalantly with each other, I have to feign a crazy interest in everything that's happening in Brussels [where Anny lived], I have to make jokes. You have to occupy yourself more with H. than with me . . . neither of us may attempt to exchange a glance other than what would be the norm in polite society."[82] He seems positively titillated by the prospect of having his wife and his lover in the same room and by the mutual role-playing that it would involve, the former supposedly oblivious of his intimacy with the latter. Yet it seems more like a game in which Helene was merely playing the role of unknowing wife. We cannot exclude the possibility that all three participants were aware of the truth but left it tactfully unmentioned for as long as the game continued. In the summer of 1933, as Berg's letters again confirm, he managed to meet both Hanna Fuchs and Edith Edwards (though presumably not at the same time).[83] If by the early 1930s Berg was writing concurrently to at least three different "lovers," real or putative (there may well have been more of whom we as yet know nothing), he must on some level have expected Helene to guess something. It is as if he were collecting simultaneous *amours* as a means of titillation in itself, his delight increasing with every new one he was able to "hide" from his wife. He even on occasion disguised his handwriting when addressing letters to his ladies (as, for example, with a letter to Edith Edwards of early 1935). Berg was thus not just a man who was unfaithful to his wife. He also took delight in being unfaithful to all the women with whom he was being unfaithful. It seems, however, that the idea of infidelity was what attracted him rather than the act itself, and one cannot but wonder if these lovers were really "lovers" at all. We know that he hardly ever met Hanna; in his letter to Edith of early 1935 he mentions that their affair had consisted of "36 hours" spent together, and his letter to Anny of March 1933 expresses disquiet that he has become fatter and less attractive in the year since she last saw him. Berg's known lovers all have one striking common denominator, namely that he hardly ever saw them, yet expended much ink in celebrating the "eternal moments" he spent with them.

Drawing parallels between life and art is a fraught enterprise, as we have seen in the other chapters of this book. But we cannot ignore the fact that Berg the constructivist composer, calculating his numbers and their multiples and manipulating his material so as to "hide" his secrets within it, was also in Berg the man. He seems to have delighted in manipulation, deception, and dissimulation, toying with secrets-that-aren't in an urge to have his secret cake and eat it in public. On the one hand, we have the careful cultivator of the political powers-that-be, trying to play the Berlin Nazis off against the Viennese Austrofascists; and on the other hand, we have the man-about-town with his compulsive lies, his calculated deceptions, his secret rendezvous, his disguised handwriting, his go-betweens and his theatrical games at afternoon teas for his wife and lovers. Yet while the reception of his music has for some thirty years been dominated by attention to Berg the supposedly secret constructivist, the biographical accounts have remained somewhat hagiographical. The aura of the angelic that his luminescent Violin Concerto bestowed on the departed Manon Gropius was after his death transferred in large part onto Berg himself, and it has not yet worn off. This process of sanctification began with Hermann Scherchen's holding up the score of the work to the public after its first performance in a gesture redolent of the presentation of the Host in a Catholic mass.[84] In his later study of Berg, Adorno's stylistic brilliance allowed him to offer vital insights while at the same time enhancing his beloved teacher's halo, all under a formidable veneer of intellectual objectivity. He even added an anecdote of Berg-as-action-hero, telling how he once saved a man from being run over by a Berlin subway train by pulling him off the tracks in the nick of time. And he praised Berg's "complete absence of authoritarianism," characterizing him as someone who "knew that death was always so close that he treated life as something provisional . . . he succeeded in never becoming an adult, without, however, remaining infantile."[85] It is as if Berg were some kind of Peter Pan—or perhaps, an angel—and in truth Berg's dedication to Manon seems to hover behind the biographical portions of Adorno's text. Adorno even manages to make Berg a victim of the Nazis, claiming that plummeting royalties in Germany had made him hesitate to pay for proper treatment of the carbuncle that killed him. Adorno's argument is not without justification, though he then half-admits that Berg was also the victim of his own inaction.[86] Berg's supposed otherworldliness can be observed in almost all retellings of his final illness. He himself mentions the initial problem in a letter to Alma as "an insect sting [*Insektenstich*] in the middle of the spine," and commentators have doggedly retained this description, ignoring the precise nature of his subsequent ailment by referring continually to a "spinal abscess" or a carbuncle "at the base of the spine," presumably because to state that he had a boil on the buttock seems too vulgar for a man supposedly grieving for an angelic dead teenager and well on his way to joining the angels himself.[87] Berg himself later used the Latin *podex*, leaving no doubt as to the seat of the problem. However, even this euphemism-that-isn't seems to cross the bounds of decorum for some German-speaking commentators, for a recent book shyly adds an endnote number to the word when it is quoted, explaining it at the back of the book as briefly as possible, as if to reduce embarrassment to a minimum: "Podex: Hinterteil" (in English: "Podex: posterior").[88]

It is human nature that our ability to empathize with a death is proportional to the degree of intimacy we have enjoyed with the deceased. As we have observed, Alma and the Bergs knew each other well, though the insistence with which Berg felt it necessary as early as 1919 to assure "Beloved Alma" that she was their "*best* friend . . . our *only* friend" (his underlining) makes it evident that it was really a rather one-sided matter.[89] The two families were in touch with each other by letter just about every month in the late 1920s and early 1930s, to judge by their extant correspondence. The Werfels divided their time between Vienna, Semmering, and Venice, and despite the continuing, frequent avowals of loving friendship to be found in Alma's correspondence with the Bergs, it is not certain just how often Alban saw Alma in person (if it were often, why would they need to correspond?). There is nothing to suggest that Berg was particularly close to Manon herself—after all, how many of us could admit to being close to the teenage children of our friends? If Berg and Manon had been close enough for him to pour out his grief for her in a Violin Concerto, surely he would have mentioned her death and his "requiem" for her in his correspondence with Schoenberg and others? Yet Manon remains all but unmentioned. In Berg's extensive extant correspondence with Schoenberg—a man who also belonged to Alma's wider circle—Manon receives just three mentions, the last of them in a letter of February 20, 1921.[90] She does not even feature in the letter quoted earlier in which Berg writes in detail of his concerto, demonstrating its note row.[91] Admittedly, at least one letter from Berg to Schoenberg from this time is no longer extant, for on November 30, 1935, he mentions his new concerto and adds that "I wrote to you back then about the commission from the Boston violinist Krasner."[92] But even if he had mentioned Manon Gropius in that lost letter, it is still strange that Berg's primary reference point for the concerto is not Manon's death, but the commission from Krasner. Nor does Berg write of Manon in his extant correspondence with Adorno or Soma Morgenstern. To the former he mentioned on July 4, 1935, "the violin concerto commissioned from me by the American violinist Louis Krasner";[93] to the latter he did not even mention the actual concerto or Krasner by name, instead praising the virtues of hard work in a letter of June 4, 1935, noting that "it is however thanks to the compulsion of the 'commission.'"[94] There remains the "official" program of the work published by Willi Reich in his article "Requiem for Manon" in the summer of 1935 and written (by his own admission) in collaboration with Berg himself.[95] But even this cannot be trusted. Reich writes that "the formal layout [*Anlage*] of the concerto was determined by the programmatic idea," though we know from the sketches that the formal layout had been decided upon at least a month before Manon's death.[96] And in fact the programmatic explanation given here refers only to "the girl," not to anyone specific. If the concerto is a "Requiem for Manon," then she is strangely absent in Berg's own discourse around it.

We might be wrong. The death of any person at the age of eighteen is a terrible thing, and Berg might have been as moved as Reich suggests he was. But the dedication of the work seems most like an attempt to keep Alma happy, with the "program" constructed around it a necessary crutch to convince her of the composer's sincerity. The absence of Manon's name in both dedication and program could have been a means of avoiding a direct lie, not unlike a child telling an untruth while crossing its fingers behind its back. The story of the work's "inspiration" is certainly a powerful one, for it deals with one of the most emotive topics of all—the death of a near-child—and also evokes the arch-romantic obsession with the transience of youth and beauty. It is a story that Berg knew would be questioned by no one and that would serve to obscure what was the real reason for the concerto's composition: the $1,500 that Krasner had promised him for it, worth some 7,000 schillings in 1935 and thus more than the annual "pension" of 500 schillings per month that Universal Edition was already paying him. Berg admitted as much to Adorno on February 19, 1935: "I *have* to 'accomplish' a commission for a violin concerto, since I need it to live."[97] A concerto "to the memory of an angel" is undoubtedly a more appealing nickname than, say, a "Dollar Concerto" might have been (we take our cue here from Kurt Atterberg's Sixth Symphony of 1927/28, nicknamed the "Dollar Symphony" after it won a hefty prize from the Columbia Graphophone Company).

If the "inspiration" for his Violin Concerto truly lay in Berg's dire finances, this tells us nothing about how Berg might have grieved (or not) at Manon's death, nor does it exclude the possibility of any other aesthetic or programmatic import. But Berg's public proclamation (through Reich) of his concerto's commemoration of the death of Manon Gropius clashes starkly with his private silence about it. This surely affords us another glimpse of the latently cruel streak that Puffett noted and that we also saw in Berg's attitude toward Schoenberg's sacking by the Nazis. For if we are correct, Berg had no compunction about using the death of a child he knew in order to manipulate the emotional response of his listeners. This, in turn, suggests that beneath the surface of his indebtedness and loving friendship toward Alma Mahler there lay an unspoken resentment, for he would otherwise surely have hesitated to lie about his response to her child's death. Berg's own death soon after the work's completion essentially placed a hermetic seal over the supposed meaning of his concerto, for it now offered a perfect contemporary example of "lateness" in music that fitted neatly with the popular narratives of his Austro-German forbears Mozart, Beethoven, and Wagner. There, lateness denoted ripeness, a full flowering of one's creative powers and somehow a sensing of death's approaching tread. The Violin Concerto as "Requiem for Manon," and by implication "for Alban," too—his having meanwhile joined her among the "angels"—has remained the dominant narrative of the work for over seventy years, repeated unquestioned in every program note and CD text and the subject even of primary school music projects.[98]

The incongruities between the Concerto's program and its content have nevertheless puzzled commentators. When reviewing two books on Berg in 1992, Michael Graubart remarked of the Carinthian folk song found in the Concerto that "[none] of the authors . . . seriously tackle[s] the extraordinary psychology of someone who can (whether or not he is thinking of the work as implicitly his own requiem) introduce a reminiscence of his own affair with a servant girl into what, explicitly, is intended as a requiem for a quite different girl."[99] And as early as 1977, in his article "The secret programme of the *Lyric Suite*," George Perle raised fundamental questions about Berg's "extraordinary" tendency to misinform about his biography.[100] Yet no one has ever doubted the official program of the Violin Concerto, probably because that would seem to call into question Berg's capacity for grief. It does not, as long as one is prepared to abandon the powerful pull of singularity of inspiration for the work. But as suggested above, it certainly does call into question his sincerity. The hunt for secrets and codes in Berg's work has served to exclude the possibilities of plurality, his play with numbers and initials and supposed messages having pushed us into affixing precise meanings. These purported meanings—especially where Hanna Fuchs is concerned—are often convincing. But the act of composition was surely for him, as for those before and after, something far more fluid. Berg did not hesitate to diverge from the rules of dodecaphony where the trajectory of his material required it, nor would he have restricted himself to single, fixed meanings in his music if a plurality of possibilities offered a more subtle means of expression.

The Concerto's links to the Austro-German tradition noted above—the thematic similarities to Brahms, the inclusion of a Bach chorale, the waltzes, the Austrian folk song, and the work's tonal references—all suggest that Berg was keen to write a work that was both accessible and insistently Austro-Germanic. Given that his music was decried as "degenerate" in Nazi Germany and he himself denounced erroneously as Jewish (therefore, in Nazi parlance, "not German"), we should not be surprised if he wanted to use his new concerto to demonstrate that a twelve-tone composer can write a largely tonal work of immediate emotional impact, one audibly in the tradition of Bach, Beethoven, Brahms, Wagner, and Mahler. There is no reason to believe that Berg felt that a rehabilitation north of the border was impossible for him, and the accessibility of the Violin Concerto reflects that. The prospect of financial ruin can wonderfully concentrate the mind.

Aside from the financial, political, and aesthetic aspects of the work's conception, there are indeed musical and numerological references in it to a woman—though not to Manon. She was by no means the only "angel" in his life. The word *Engel* features prominently in another of his works of this time, namely *Lulu*, when the Countess Geschwitz sings her last words: "Lulu! My angel! Let me see you once more! I am close to you! I will stay close to you—in eternity!" The final chord of the opera is based on the initials of Alban and Hanna, and Berg wrote the score with a pen that she had given him. If these last bars of *Lulu* refer to any specific "angel," then it must be to Hanna.[101] Let us not forget that Berg called Hanna his "immortal beloved" in his first extant love letter to her of July 23, 1925, in reference to Beethoven's famous letter—a letter that itself begins "My angel, my all, my very self"; and "Engel" is also how Wagner refers repeatedly to Mathilde

Wesendonck—indeed, it is the final word of his "farewell letter" to her of July 6, 1858, that Berg seems to paraphrase in his own "farewell letter" to Hanna of November 16, 1926, as we have noted above.

In his last surviving letter to Hanna, written in late 1934 just after this final scene of *Lulu* had received its first performance in Berlin, Berg pondered wistfully the approach of their tenth "anniversary" in May 1935 (note that number 10 again), lamenting how little they had seen each other in recent times. He all but admits that their "affair" can never be rekindled. In his letter to Krasner of March 28, 1935, he wrote that he was going to the Wörthersee in May to write his concerto; and since that was a place that by his own admission he associated directly with Hanna,[102] it would be logical to assume that he planned to celebrate her and their never-to-be-rekindled affair in the work he was planning to write at the time of their tenth "anniversary." This also suggests that the insistence in the literature that Berg had found work on the concerto difficult before Manon's death is also inaccurate, the result no doubt of an undue focus on that event as his "inspiration." As mentioned above, the outline of the work had been sketched by late March, and Berg expressly told Krasner that he did not intend to start work until May, when he would be out of Vienna. Hanna's initials (HF, in English B♮ and F) play a pivotal role in the row of the Violin Concerto and the work's structure is obviously built upon multiples of 23 and 10, those numbers associated by Berg with himself and Hanna. Even the chain of thirds in the note row might be a reference to Hanna, for Berg derived similar chains of thirds from permutations of his row for the *Lyric Suite* (as he himself mentioned in a letter to Schoenberg of July 13, 1926) and of his row for the concert aria *Der Wein*, both of which were indisputably inspired by Hanna (the row for the Concerto is to be found, for example, in similar form—albeit incomplete and in transposition—in the cello part from the fourth bar onward of the fifth movement of the *Lyric Suite*; see ex. 3.5).[103]

A chain of thirds might signify nothing more than a chain of thirds—we again risk an act of overinterpretation. Nevertheless, everything that we know of the Violin Concerto's structure points to it being primarily a reflection of Berg's continuing obsession with Hanna. If he indeed felt that the tenth anniversary of their meeting also signified de facto the end of their affair, then a concerto "in memory of an angel" written largely in that month must surely refer to her. It would explain the avoidance of Manon's name in both the program and the dedication and also the expression mark "amoroso" to be found in the concerto's chorale variations (hardly appropriate in a requiem for a friend's young

daughter). If one reads Reich's program in this light, then one is struck
not just by its refusal to acknowledge Manon, but by its lack of any
specific reference to illness or decease. It can be read just as well as a
metaphorical narrative of a love affair whose passion has been extin-
guished. Reich even offers a direct link to Hanna by stating that aspects
of the Concerto "are reminiscent of the unfolding of the *Lyric Suite*,
with which the concerto shares the qualification as a 'latent drama,' as
it also has much of its atmosphere [*Ton*] in common."[104] And if Hanna
"is" the work's program, then Reich's statement in his article about "the
formal layout" being "determined by the programmatic idea" is no longer mendacious. Even that Carinthian folk song could refer to Hanna,
for in its most prominent appearance (see ex. 3.6) its refrain is a prolonged doodle around "her" notes, B♮ (here as C♭ in violin and trumpet) and F. If Berg found the tune attractive and its tale of illicit sex
appealing, then there is no reason to assume that its mention of a name
other than "Hanna" would have prevented him from using it. (Hanna is
not a common name in the Austrian provinces, so he would probably
never have found any tune, Carinthian or otherwise, that mentions it.)
If Berg did find the reference to "Miazzl" a serendipitous reminder of
his teenage liaison, it could have been for him an added layer of meaning, not a *raison d'être* for the tune's inclusion. The same might be said
of his choice of chorale for the latter section of the Concerto.

The cantata from which Berg took his chorale—*O Ewigkeit, du
Donnerwort*—deserves a final mention. It was apparently Oskar
Kokoschka's favorite, and in 1914 he had used it as the basis for a series of
eleven lithographs entitled *Bachkantate* in which he endeavored to come to
terms with his disastrous affair with Alma and her abortion of their child.
Kokoschka later claimed that his friend Leo Kestenberg had explained
the cantata to him at the piano;[105] though since Kokoschka was in Vienna
in April 1914, it is possible that he and Berg also attended the same performance of the cantata in that month under Siegfried Ochs. Bach's religious text is transformed by Kokoschka into an autobiographical drama
with the artist and Alma as the protagonists. The final lithograph, entitled
"Pièta ('Es ist genug')" depicts a grieving Alma with Kokoschka dead in
her lap, a handkerchief pressed to her mouth (see fig. 3.4). There can be
little doubt that Berg was acquainted with the lithographs, given that they
were widely disseminated in three editions (including a "Volksausgabe"—a
cheap "popular edition" in 1918/19) and that he had known both Alma and
Kokoschka since before the First World War.[106] Kokoschka in later years
referred to Berg as a "friend of my youth."[107]

Example 3.5. Berg, *Lyric Suite*, 5th movement, mm. 1–7; note the chain of thirds in the cello.

The correspondence between the first notes of the chorale and the last notes of Berg's tone row may have been the determining factor in Berg's choice of chorale for his Concerto, but the added resonance of the Kokoschka/Alma connection must have intrigued him. Kokoschka's lithographs implicitly depict Alma as a failed mother responsible for the death of their child. Since Berg must have been aware of the significance of "Es ist genug" in Alma's biography, to use it in a concerto that is supposedly a "requiem" for another of her children suggests once more a degree of callousness on his part. Particularly significant for our reading of the concerto, however, is the fact that Kokoschka sexualizes Bach's cantata, turning it into a doomed love affair in which the man is the abandoned party—much as we have argued here that Berg's concerto thematizes the dying of his affair with Hanna (let us not forget that marking "amoroso"). As Paul Bekker observed not long after the publication of the lithographs, the cantata in Kokoschka's hands becomes an "erotic mysterium."[108] Berg's mention of *Stöhnen* (groaning) and *Seufzen* (sighs) in his sketches for the concerto, along with his insistence on the word *Höhepunkt* (climax) in his score can also be interpreted in a sexual manner that arguably makes more sense than any other interpretation. This does not explain Berg's having written *Lähmungsakkord*—the "chord of paralysis"—in the sketches at the point he later designated as *Höhepunkt*. It might have been meant as a metaphor for

Figure 3.4. Oskar Kokoschka, *Pietà ('Es ist genug')—Bach Cantata*, lithograph, 1916–17. © Fondation Oskar Kokoschka / 2014, ProLitteris, Zurich. Reproduced with permission.

his lovelorn state, or it might indeed have referred to Manon, or both. Just because we here interpret the Concerto as primarily a testament to Berg's love for Hanna Fuchs does not mean that his imagination afforded her exclusive rights to every note he wrote. Perhaps at some point while making his sketches after April 22, 1935, he sincerely contemplated the notion of commemorating Manon in the work, and perhaps some element of that intent remained—if primarily as a metaphor for his own loss of Hanna as signified by those 10s and 23s.

All in all: if there really is a "secret" behind the Violin Concerto, it is that there probably is none. On the one hand, it is a work written for money and situated intentionally in the accessible Austro-German tradition of Beethoven and Brahms, and on the other hand, it is just as openly obsessed with Hanna Fuchs as were the works that preceded it. Nevertheless, we should not let ourselves be led into replacing one straightforward tale of inspiration with another. Our appreciation of the Concerto can only be enhanced by recognizing the plurality of factors—private, public, political, and economic—that impinged upon its conception and composition. For these were always there; only the aura of Manon-as-angel has prevented us from seeing the obvious.

Example 3.6. Berg, Violin Concerto, first movement, mm. 220–27 (strings and woodwind omitted). Note Berg's "doodle" around the notes H (= B natural/C flat) and F in the last two measures.

CHAPTER FOUR

WILHELM FURTWÄNGLER AND THE RETURN OF THE MUSE

The creative silences of artists have been a matter of continuing fascination for the past two hundred years. Pondering the drying up of the springs of inspiration—Samuel Taylor Coleridge's manic-depressive blocks, Harper Lee's withdrawal after the *Mockingbird*, Salinger's post-*Rye*-catching seclusion—seems to have an appeal equal to that of pondering them when fully flowing. Our postromantic world still tends to view the source of inspiration as mysterious and unknowable, but its inverse, a creative block, seems by contrast to be finite and thus more easily comprehensible. Hunting for the source of the Nile is a strenuous exercise that must end inconclusively in muddy mountain marshes in the Congo. But there is little that is inconclusive about it when it hits the Aswan Dam.

Creative blocks occurred long before Coleridge and others declared their blockedness, but there seems to have been no general awareness of their existence before the late eighteenth century allowed creativity to leave the realm of artisanship for that of high art. There are innumerable medical and psychological explanations for writer's block in the literature today, but there are no records of J. S. Bach telling his employers that he couldn't write next Sunday's cantata because he was feeling a little bipolar, just as Haydn presumably never told his employer Prince Esterházy that he couldn't dash off his hundred-and-somethingth baryton trio because he felt his defenses crumbling against an oral-masochistic conflict.[1] As soon as artists had to be "inspired," however, they found that they could also be uninspired.

In the world of music, the most famous silent composers were Gioachino Rossini, who wrote almost nothing in the thirty-odd years after his *Guillaume Tell*, and Jean Sibelius, who fell silent after his Seventh Symphony (though there are reports that an Eighth was all but completed until put to a fiery end by the composer himself). Rossini had been a workaholic, but after *Guillaume Tell* he acquired the financial means to abandon his work and relax and eat instead, and so he did. Sibelius, on the other hand, was an alcoholic, and this presumably played a role in his silence. Other composers have been creatively becalmed for shorter or longer periods. Richard Wagner famously composed almost nothing in the five years after *Lohengrin*, though he channeled his creativity instead into a wealth of autobiographical and theoretical writings that led directly to his *Rheingold*, written in full torrent in late 1853 and early 1854 and followed almost immediately by the *Walküre*, its composer's swiftness being more than matched by the strength of his inspiration.

There are, however, few cases of composers abandoning composition for over a decade and then returning to it. Closer to our own time, there are two examples. One is Rolf Liebermann, who after much success with orchestral works and operas, devoted his energies instead to music management, first as Intendant of the Hamburg Opera, then in the equivalent position at the Paris Opéra and finally back in his old job in Hamburg again. Between 1966 and 1981 he apparently wrote nothing, but after his retirement he devoted his final years largely to composition. An even more extreme case is that of Wilhelm Furtwängler, who after completing his Te Deum in 1909 at the age of twenty-three produced nothing for the next twenty-six years until his Piano Quintet, dated 1935. The floodgates now opened, and by the time of his death in 1954 Furtwängler had also written two violin sonatas, a piano concerto, and three symphonies. Since the average length of each of these works is an hour, and his orchestral works are scored for large forces, seven works in nineteen years is a thoroughly decent output, especially if one considers that the previous two-and-a-half decades had produced nothing at all. When one takes into account Furtwängler's strenuous conducting commitments and the fact that these nineteen years of creativity spanned the Second World War and a period of recurrent ill health after it, then we must admit that Furtwängler's muse was remarkably faithful when she finally deigned to return.

That return of the muse coincides with a singular event in Furtwängler's biography—so conveniently, in fact, that an assumption of causality seems inevitable. This was his resignation from his official posts on December 4, 1934, in the wake of the so-called Hindemith Case, when his open defense of the composer Paul Hindemith and his music resulted in Furtwängler becoming temporarily non grata with the Nazis (for Hitler detested Hindemith). Besides abandoning his position as chief conductor of the Berlin Philharmonic, Furtwängler also gave up the vice-presidency of the *Reichsmusikkammer* (a Nazi body ostensibly intended to oversee all musical matters in the Third Reich, but which remained in purpose undefined and in impact limited). On December 10, 1934, Furtwängler wrote to his longstanding friend John Knittel: "I resigned all my positions as conductor a few days ago. I have been through all kinds of commotion but nevertheless, the whole thing has its good side: now I have *time*, and so I'm pondering whether I might not accept for a while your often-expressed invitation to visit you in Egypt. . . . For me it's primarily a matter of advancing my other musical work (compositions) in this time."[2]

In 1979, Furtwängler's widow confirmed in her reminiscences that it was only after withdrawing from his official posts that Furtwängler had found the necessary time "to complete works already begun, and begin new ones."[3] She had not known him in 1934/35, so it was presumably the reason he himself gave her. There is probably more than a grain of truth in it. According to René Trémine's chronological listing of Furtwängler's conducting activities, he did not conduct between December 2, 1934, and April 12, 1935, when he resumed work again with the Berlin Philharmonic.[4] This was now in a freelance capacity, a fact that Furtwängler would repeatedly point out after the War, as he felt that it absolved him of responsibility for (artistic) decisions in the Reich with which he could not agree.

One theory that has appealed to Furtwängler apologists is that of so-called inner emigration, a term used for artists who remained in Nazi Germany but adopted a stance of passive opposition to the regime.[5] The staple example given in music is Karl Amadeus Hartmann, who wrote for his desk drawer and did not perform his works in Germany while the Nazis were in power. In Furtwängler's case, his dispute with the Nazi regime is supposed to have prompted his retreat from the tribulations of everyday life into a safer inner world where he could voice his feelings through his art alone.[6] While it is not impossible that Furtwängler came to believe this himself, it does not correspond wholly to the facts, for his return to work in April 1935 de facto also meant his "rehabilitation." When he conducted the Berlin Philharmonic again in Berlin, on May 3, 1935, the concert was attended by Hitler, Goering, and Goebbels. Hitler made a point of shaking Furtwängler's hand in public where the cameras could see them.

The next season, 1935/36, Furtwängler conducted some hundred performances in total (in the concert hall and in the opera house); his conducting career was more or less back to normal. He did squeeze in a three-week holiday with Knittel in Egypt in March 1936, and then—with Hitler's express permission—he took off the winter of the season after that, from the beginning of August 1936 to the end of January 1937, to work on his compositions. The 1937/38 season, however, saw him giving around a hundred performances again, a number he almost reached in the next season, too. Furtwängler's works of this period are not dated precisely. The manuscript of his First Violin Sonata bears various dates from the year 1935, whereas the proofs give 1936 as its year of completion; the Second Violin Sonata, however, we can be relatively sure dates from 1938–39—thus from a time when Furtwängler was as busy as ever on the podium. In fact, as Trémine's list makes evident, Furtwängler had long before his squabble with Hitler enjoyed occasional extensive breaks between conducting engagements, such as in 1926 (nothing between June 2 and September 21—thus three-and-a-half months free) or in 1930 (nothing from July 1 to September 30—three months free). If Furtwängler wasn't conducting at a festival, then a summer break of between eight and twelve weeks was nothing unusual.

It is not for us to suggest that Furtwängler should have been spending his summers composing instead of relaxing or riding or pursuing his other pastimes. Yet we cannot accept at face value the argument that he composed nothing for twenty-five years because he did not have the time to do so, especially since he managed to write a forty-five-minute violin sonata in 1938/39 when he had as little time spare as had ever been the case. Furthermore, his archives are brimful of musical sketches from the years before 1935. The date of composition of his Piano Quintet used to be given as 1935, but in fact there are sketches for it from as early as 1912. The first Violin Sonata, previously dated 1934/35, was begun in around 1916; the Symphonic Concerto for Piano and Orchestra, completed in 1937, was begun about 1920; and most remarkable of all is the genesis of his First Symphony, once dated 1937–40 but whose beginnings date back to 1905. Furtwängler had always had time to compose; he just had not been able to finish anything. So when he claimed to have had more time from 1935 onward, what he seems to have meant was more a matter of mental space in which to work, rather than anything measurable in minutes, hours, days, or weeks.

If we are to understand both Furtwängler's return to composing and the silence that preceded it, we must first make a closer investigation of his earlier period of composition, namely the years up to his Te Deum of 1909. Furtwängler was privately educated. His father Adolf was a renowned, wealthy archaeologist and was determined to give his children a first-class, humanistic, liberal education. Music lessons were naturally a part of this, and Furtwängler seems to have begun composing almost as soon as he began playing the piano. His earliest "work" is a little song entitled "Ein Stückchen von den Tieren" (A little piece about the animals) that his mother helped him write down and that was a birthday present for his father on June 30, 1893, when Furtwängler was seven. Many more little songs, piano pieces, and chamber music works exist from the years thereafter, some bearing "official" opus numbers. They are without exception weak, full of diluted Schubert and Beethoven. Since several of the songs have been released on CD nevertheless, one can judge them for oneself.[7] When Furtwängler was in his teens, his father Adolf engaged the composers Josef Rheinberger and Max von Schillings as composition tutors, though they seem to have had little positive impact. The Three Piano Pieces of 1902/3 are the earliest work by Furtwängler for which an occasional airing would not be an embarrassment. His first orchestral work predates them—an Overture in E-flat Major for orchestra with double wind and brass from 1899, which for a thirteen-year-old is not incompetent, but which by any objective criteria must be judged incoherent and derivative. It shows an obsession with sequence that would remain a characteristic of Furtwängler's work for the years to come. It was never performed in his lifetime, but has nevertheless been recorded since in all its awfulness.[8]

It is not clear which was the first of Furtwängler's orchestral works to be performed, but we do know that the first performance came about through his maternal uncle, Georg Dohrn, who was music director in the Silesian city of Breslau (today's Wrocław in Poland). A festschrift for the Breslau orchestra published in 1912 listed a performance on March 4, 1903, of a brief work by Furtwängler to a text from Goethe: "Schwindet, ihr dunklen Wölbungen" for chorus (SATB) and orchestra.[9] However, the review of the concert in the *Breslauer Zeitung* of March 6 made no mention of the piece, which means either that it was passed over in silence (presumably as a favor to Georg Dohrn, whose reputation would not have been enhanced by it) or that a performance was planned, perhaps even prepared and advertised but then canceled, possibly at a late stage. That would have allowed a mention of it to remain in the records later consulted by the author of the festschrift.

Half a year later, however, uncle Dohrn did indeed put a work by his nephew on one of his programs: the Symphony in D Major, written in 1902/3. The orchestration is not over-large by the standards of the day, but bigger than that of his earlier overture, with three bassoons, contrabassoon, and four horns. Only the first movement survives whole, though this alone lasts nearly twenty minutes. Emil Bohn, the critic of the *Breslauer Zeitung*, wrote about it in his review of November 6, 1903:

> Would the symphony . . . have been different, better, more unified, if its composer had let it rest a few years more in his desk drawer and then reworked it thoroughly?—Who can tell. . . . The whole symphony is, to be brief, a fruitless struggle between great desire and insufficient ability. . . . Furtwängler works in fits and starts. If he has an idea, he drags it through thick and thin and expands it so much that you'd think he could explode the heavens with it; in a trice, the moment is reached where one believes the catastrophe to be unavoidable. But he never gets beyond this point; suddenly, without any apparent reason, he breaks off. And that is what happens with every idea he has.

The critic of the *Breslauer General-Anzeiger* ("K.M.") wrote on the same day:

> This, [Furtwängler's] first symphony, is a peculiar work. In the first movement, the composer shows himself to be in a mood that is pathetic, but also asthmatic . . . After brief melodic oases one travels on through vast deserts . . . his symphony was greeted with more whistling than applause . . . He should sit down, study hard at modern instrumentation from Berlioz to Richard Strauss, and then go and write a better symphony.

And Ernst Flügel of the *Schlesische Zeitung* wrote, also on November 6:

> The third orchestral society's concert [of the season] opened with a symphony by Wilhelm Furtwängler that was rejected out of hand by the audience. Time and again in the interval one could hear in the foyer that no work had ever been rejected in such a manner throughout the whole history of the orchestra. Who is Wilhelm Furtwängler? [His] Symphony is in its individual movements and as a whole impossible to enjoy. It is not a work that is completely without talent, but it is merely the product of a hardworking, ambitious beginner who has misunderstood Brahms and Liszt.

The composer was present and had to bear the full brunt of the audience's catcalls. Furtwängler's father was also there, but was at least as convinced of his son's genius as was the son himself, and so ascribed the abject failure to everything but the work's utter absence of quality. Ernst Flügel, he was sure, had a grudge against Dohrn and had used "Willi" merely as an ersatz to get at his real enemy.[10] But if anything, the critics were generous. The work is truly awful, as can be heard from the currently available recording of its first movement.[11] The best moments are no more than undigested, half-remembered remnants of other composers. Bohn's account of ideas either worked to death or abandoned for no reason is depressingly accurate.

Just over two years later, after a brief stint as *répétiteur* with his uncle in Breslau, Furtwängler made his public debut as a conductor. He hired the Kaim Orchestra in Munich (the forerunner of today's Munich Philharmonic) and on February 19, 1906, conducted Beethoven's *Consecration of the House* overture, Bruckner's Ninth Symphony, and an Adagio for orchestra (in other sources named a "symphonic poem") that he had composed himself. It was this Adagio that Furtwängler spent the following thirty-five years reworking into the first movement of his Symphony in B Minor. In his review of March 7, 1906, for the journal *Signale für musikalische Welt*, Eugen Schmitz wrote of the Adagio as follows: "His symphonic poem in B minor that he performed for us is a remarkable test of his talent, and proof that this young musician has learnt much already. However, this overlong and formally diffuse piece does not deserve to be called a work of art."[12]

Furtwängler's conducting career began in earnest later that year when he was engaged as third kapellmeister at the Zurich City Theater and was allowed in the course of the season to conduct the odd performance of incidental music and over half a dozen performances of Léhar's *Merry Widow*. He thereafter returned to Munich where he worked as a *répétiteur* under Felix Mottl before taking up a position as third kapellmeister under Hans Pfitzner in Strasbourg in September 1910. Two months later, his uncle Dohrn stuck his neck out one last time for his composing nephew when he conducted his latest work, a Te Deum for four soloists, mixed chorus, and large orchestra on November 16 in Breslau. The reviewers were hardly more sympathetic than they had been seven years earlier. Ernst Flügel remarked how much courage it must have taken to bring out another work by the same composer after the utter failure of his earlier attempt. Without mentioning the family connection between composer and conductor, he commented that the grounds for performing the work must have been personal, for they could not have been musical. Paul Wittmann in the *Breslauer Zeitung* was blunt and unwittingly echoed the review of Furtwängler's Adagio four years earlier: "[The Te Deum] shows [Furtwängler's] infancy so clearly in his struggle with form and with his vocal and instrumental forces . . . that we cannot . . . dare to call it a 'work of art.'"

There is no doubt that the young Furtwängler had a healthy belief in his own genius—having a father even more convinced of it must have helped—but to have one's music savaged on the mere three occasions that it is performed over some seven years would be devastating to anyone. It is probably here that we should look for a reason as to why Furtwängler was unable to bring any work to completion for the next twenty-five years. Until the end of his life, he had a fear of performing his music in public. At a performance of his Second Symphony after the Second World War, he told his wife that, whenever he conducted a work of his own, he felt like "a sixteen-year-old girl who had to undress in front of a bunch of dirty old men" (an odd but telling simile, given his own lifelong, voracious appetite for young women).[13]

Furtwängler's letters over the next years repeatedly mention his composing—thus, for example, he wrote from St. Moritz on September 3, 1923, to Edith Curtius, the wife of his former tutor Ludwig, that "I have worked on all kinds of things, better than in the last 13 years (since the Te Deum). But I have to have time, time";[14] and on July 27, 1930, he wrote from Bansin to John Knittel of his Piano Concerto, "on which I have been working for several years—I *have* to finish it this time. I feel that I won't get around to it otherwise; there were already too many interruptions for too long . . . if it continues like this I have good reason to think that it will be finished by the end of August."[15] It wasn't, for it took over six years more. And in the summer of 1931, he wrote to Ludwig Curtius of his "suffering" as an "artist"—meaning as a composer—affirming that he remained as convinced of the rightness of his calling as he had been at the age of twenty, and remarking that "it was probably the greatest mistake in my life that fate and career chained me to Berlin, whereas in solitude I could have become what I believed I should become," that is, a composer.[16]

When one considers that less than a week after his enforced resignation, Furtwängler was able to write to John Knittel (as quoted above) that "the whole thing has its good side: now I have *time* . . . [for] my other musical work (compositions)," it almost seems as if his dogged defense of Hindemith in late 1934 was in some way intended to provoke the authorities into forcing upon him what he could not bring himself to do freely: to give up his conducting posts and grant himself the "solitude" that he needed to compose. In objective terms, Furtwängler in the second half of 1934 had everything that an ambitious man could have wished for. He had been chief conductor of the Leipzig Gewandhaus and Vienna Philharmonic

Orchestras; he was City General Music Director in Berlin, the chief conductor of the Berlin Philharmonic, director of the Berlin State Opera, vice-
president of the Reichsmusikkammer and celebrated in the press as the
"Führer of our Philharmonic."[17] Probably not even Richard Strauss had as
much power as he did. "Monopoleon" was Furtwängler's nickname among
his peers, and justly so, for his talent was matched by an immense ambi-
tion that had seen all its goals realized bar one.[18] Perhaps in some corner of
his mind, Furtwängler had decided that the prospect of achieving that last
goal was worth giving up everything else—or perhaps he felt that giving up
everything else was somehow a prerequisite for achieving it. And perhaps
even, at the back of his mind, the fact that potential replacements such as
Otto Klemperer, Bruno Walter, and Paul Kletzki were all in exile made
him think he was irreplaceable—if he were to abandon the podium for any
length of time, he would soon be begged back anyway.

By late 1934, two other factors had come into play that would as-
sist Furtwängler in realizing his aim to compose freely again. Music
of a modernist slant had by now been largely forbidden by the Nazis.
Just five days after Furtwängler published his November 25 defense of
Hindemith in the *Deutsche Allgemeine Zeitung* (in an article entitled
"The Hindemith Case"), Erich Kleiber conducted the world première
of Alban Berg's *Lulu Suite* in Berlin. This proved a step too far for the
Nazis and resulted in both Kleiber's exile and the banning of Berg's
music in the Reich. With Schoenberg long gone and Hindemith and
Berg to all intents and purposes removed from the scene, there were no
modernist composers left with any real voice in Germany. Furtwängler's
failed defense of a "modernist" composer in fact helped to prepare the
ground for his own forthcoming composing successes, for the kind of
neo-Brucknerian music that Furtwängler wanted to write was now sty-
listically and politically acceptable.

Furthermore, the critics had been muzzled. It is quite possible that this
was the prime factor in affording Furtwängler the psychological space that
he needed to be "inspired" again, and to have the courage to perform his
works. If the regime favored him, then no journalist would dare to criticize
his music; if the regime were against him, then he could claim adverse political motivation for any bad reviews and feel justified in ignoring them.
Seen in this light, it is probably no coincidence that it was not after he re-
linquished his posts that Furtwängler completed his long-begun works and
wrote new ones, but after his de facto rehabilitation by the Nazis less than
three months later. The first performance of any of his new works, that of
his First Violin Sonata, took place on March 4, 1937, and the reviews were

indeed good. Since Furtwängler had ostensibly never doubted the wrongness of his critics in their rejection of his music—as he implied clearly in the letter to Curtius quoted above—he had no reason to doubt the honesty of the critics now that they favored him, for they merely confirmed what he already believed.

The Nazi attitude toward music critics received official confirmation in Goebbels's official ban on art "criticism" on November 26, 1936, when he insisted that reviewers in the arts should in future "describe" works and "honor" them [Würdigung], leaving the formation of an opinion on them to the public itself. To his credit, Furtwängler was one of the few who made clear to Goebbels his dislike of the ban.[19] One could interpret this either as a generous act founded on a sense of moral and artistic decency or as a self-serving gesture to massage his conscience in the knowledge that such a protest would have no impact anyway. The truth, as so often with Furtwängler, lies somewhere between the two extremes, just one of many instances of contradictory behavior from a man given to extreme vacillation, always wanting to have his cake and eat it. Indeed, one could argue that in the late 1930s, Furtwängler had the best of all worlds. He was no longer bound by administrative ties to any orchestra or institution, but was nevertheless able to continue his career as chief conductor of the Berlin Philharmonic in all but name. He was *persona grata* in a one-party state, yet under no compulsion to join its party or to take on any office that he did not want. He could remain—or imagine that he remained—aloof from any of the messy political/aesthetic decisions that the Nazis made, while at the same time occupying a position in which to profit from them. He remained as influential and as wealthy as before; he was able to protest at the enforced complacency of the critics while at the same time benefitting from it, just as he would try to protect individual Jews while remaining a servant of the very state hell-bent on exterminating them. His ambivalence is well illustrated by his refusal to conduct at the Nazi Party's Nuremberg Party Congress in 1938, but his readiness instead to conduct on the eve of it—a festive performance of Wagner's *Meistersinger* with the ensemble of the Vienna State Opera (just six months after Austria had been incorporated by force into the Reich). To the rest of the world and to posterity—and, no doubt, to the Nazis—conducting on the eve of the Congress was no different from conducting at it. But to Furtwängler, it seems, the difference was real and crucial.

Furtwängler's endeavor to revive his composing career even seems written into the fabric of his music that emerged after that long creative hibernation. The opening of his Piano Quintet can serve as an aural metaphor

Example 4.1. Furtwängler, opening of the first movement of the Piano Quintet (1935), mm. 1–18. © Ries & Erler, Berlin. Reproduced with permission.

for his struggle to regain his muse, consisting as it does of a single gesture that begins questioningly in the strings on an offbeat and is answered immediately in imposing fashion by the piano with an upward swirl. But this opening gesture is repeated and turns back on itself, as if in an act of despair at an inability to find a suitable continuation. The sense of emphatic desperation is underlined here by the insistent use of double accents coupled with the instruction "marc.[ato]" where single accents would do, and by the repeated use of crescendo markings despite the strings playing *ff* from the beginning, the piano *fff*, with not a decrescendo anywhere in sight (see ex. 4.1).

Furtwängler's thematic material can sound imposing, but as Roman Brotbeck has remarked, Furtwängler avoids developing his thematic material, debases the few moments of beauty in his music by repeating them, and tries to attain monumentalism by sheer repetition.[20] It is as if while composing Furtwängler were imagining himself on the podium, arriving to tumultuous applause and plunging the audience into his music with a spectacular opening sweep—but then his fear that what follows might prove a failure leaves his imagination frozen in this one moment and drives him to repeat it over and again. As Brotbeck has observed, Furtwängler's scores are littered with detailed, poetic expression and tempo markings that seem to serve as an ersatz for the poeticism they try in vain to conjure up in the music itself.[21]

The First Violin Sonata begins not dissimilarly to the Quintet. The piano accompaniment offers a wash of septuplets that obscure any sense of meter, and above them the violin's initial theme (almost an inversion of the opening theme of the Quintet) enters hesitantly, its syncopations all but inaudible to the listener because the accompaniment offers no resistance to them. Instead of leading us somewhere, the composer resorts again to sequence, and the impression conveyed is one of ambivalence and indecision. There is here a certain resemblance to the banal monumentalism of Nazi aesthetics—why bother to design a twenty-meter triumphal arch if one can build it five times as high at ten times the cost?—though while such a similarity in intent can offer a reason why Furtwängler's bombast might have appealed in Nazi Germany, it would be unjust to see any direct causal relationship here. Such bombast is just as obvious in his early music and survived into the works he wrote after the Second World War.

Only Furtwängler's Second Symphony, written in 1944/45, succeeds in attaining some of the grandeur it claims for itself, and it has found a number of adherents. But not even the advocacy of Edwin Fischer or Daniel Barenboim has managed to bring the Symphonic Concerto for piano into

the normal concert repertoire. It is tempting to see a direct corollary between Furtwängler the man and Furtwängler the composer, as the former's
hesitant, vacillating stance in the Third Reich seems reflected with remarkable immediacy in his music. Similar tendencies can be observed in his
writings on music too, for his prose also often circles around what he wants
to say, and numerous versions exist of certain writings that seem to repre-
sent stages not of increasing precision of thought, but rather multiple levels
of vacillation.[22] But again, we must be wary of putting carts before horses,
as Furtwängler's pre-1933 writings are hardly more cogent than those from
after 1945.

Once returned, Furtwängler's muse never left him again. We do not
know whether or not he feared she might, but his last article—written
shortly before his death in November 1954—can offer us certain insights
into his attitude toward her. It was published posthumously as *Der Musiker
und sein Publikum*. Much of this article is given over to criticism of atonality and its proponents (especially Schoenberg) who have, he maintains,
broken with all tradition, annulled the age-old compact between the artist
and his public, and returned Western music to a chaos akin to the "innumerable negro drums" of a nocturnal "African jungle."[23] In pre-atonal
days, he says, young composers who did not succeed immediately in win-
ning the favor of the public had risked being "cast onto the dung heap."[24]
However, the atonalists have not only made composing "easy" again,[25] but
have also created an atmosphere in which young composers are no longer
subject to a "struggle for existence" and in which the "ideology of the time"
and the "propaganda of the progressives" have allowed atonal composers
to achieve rapid, unearned success.[26] Even if one acknowledges that the
mores of the day allowed for terminology we now find objectionable, and
even if we accept that Furtwängler's similes and metaphors aim to depict an
incomprehensible, foreign other for which the "dark continent" was merely
a long-standing cipher in the West, his prose is still surprising in its brutality and lack of self-reflection. In one dreadful moment, Furtwängler goes
so far as to compare the modernists to Goebbels.[27] Even darkest Africa was
as a simile not other enough for him.

"Of the fate of those . . . who only content themselves with writing music—perhaps rather good music—I will say nothing," he writes (implicitly of himself), but then proceeds to say rather a lot about "them" anyway: "They are today—regardless of whatever they want to be—deader
than dead."[28] Having rejected the "path of chaos" and withstood the "poi-
son of today's music," these "real" composers must struggle to be heard
at all. Furtwängler does not mention Pfitzner here, though their views

are strikingly similar. Like Pfitzner in his own writings on inspiration,[29] Furtwängler lumps together atonalists, theorists, and all those who purportedly ignore or reject the "mystery of artistic creation."[30] He holds up Mozart, Beethoven, Schubert, and Wagner as examples of composers who achieved greatness through the music they wrote, not (he says) by profiting from the propaganda of an aesthetically progressive ideological clique. It is clear that they here all stand for one specific contemporary composer: Furtwängler himself. As a young man he had indeed landed on the "dung heap" with his music, he had indeed undergone a "struggle for existence," and his lack of success as a composer is implicitly explained away here as resulting precisely from the actual aesthetic value of his creations.

One can excuse these extraordinary statements as the rantings of an aging man already in failing health who feels that the world has passed him by. He was neither the first nor the last artist who with increasing years propagated an ossified, conservative aesthetic, who looked back in anger at all he felt he had been prevented from achieving, and who regarded askance the apparent ease with which youth asserted itself. Yet as we have seen, Furtwängler's aesthetic had barely changed over the years. And unlike the younger composers who supposedly "had it easy," his position at the head of the world's most famous orchestra meant that he could perform his own compositions in the world's finest venues without having to worry about being landed with an unsympathetic conductor or an incompetent orchestra. That is a rare privilege for any composer. The attitude of the critics toward Furtwängler's music in fact remained largely positive after the Second World War. He could not claim to have suddenly become a composing pariah consigned to the dung heap again, though his writings imply that he had. His extreme statements seem to have offered him a kind of self-protection: if his music was rejected, then it was not because it was bad, but because it was good and because the music world had been polluted by ideology and propaganda (words he had no doubt internalized during the thousand-year Reich between 1933 and 1945). But Furtwängler seems to be more than merely second-guessing his possible critics. For if the path of a true composer is one of struggle, and if Furtwängler in objective terms has nothing more to struggle against (thanks to the continuing strength of his reputation and his position of power in the music world), then he needed to invent a struggle—not merely to justify the existence of his own music, but to create the conditions in which it could be composed.

Furtwängler was not the first composer who seemed to need strife in order to compose, nor the first to create such strife if it were absent. Ulrich Drüner has suggested convincingly that Wagner was just such a case, and that, for example, his republication of his anti-Semitic tract *Jewishness in Music* in 1869 should be seen in this regard. It was a well-nigh self-destructive act at the time, though Drüner suggests that the resultant controversy was precisely what Wagner needed to kick-start his muse when taking up his work once more on the *Ring of the Nibelung* after a hiatus of more than a decade.[31] If we view Furtwängler in a similar light, it can help to explain both his long silence as a composer and his sudden ability to return to composition in 1935. His conducting career had taken off at the same moment that his composing career plunged into oblivion. His years in Lübeck and Mannheim were the start of a rapid trajectory of success that took him to the pinnacle of his profession with the orchestras of Berlin and Leipzig by his late thirties. As we have observed above, he subsequently consolidated his position until he was essentially the most powerful musician in all Germany. His strife with Goebbels and the Nazis was the first professional setback of any consequence that he had endured since the failure of his early compositions. Perhaps the one struggle somehow prompted memories of the other, but in any case it does seem that it was this new struggle that set free his creativity once again. Furtwängler's semirehabilitation in mid-1935 by no means resolved his conflict with Goebbels, as all the documents confirm. But if their conflict stimulated his muse, then his rehabilitation—as already postulated above—will have provided at least the necessary cushion from a potentially critical press.

It was thus not the fact of having "more time" that allowed Furtwängler to compose—this being something of a fallacy, as we have seen—but it might have been instead the fact that he now had a source of friction to act as a creative stimulus, while at the same time he no longer needed to fear public criticism of the notes he wrote. That source of friction naturally disappeared in 1945, though Furtwängler's need for it did not. So a new conflict had to be found instead. His aesthetic had barely changed since his youth, remaining conservative and Brucknerian throughout, and his concert programming had always been dominated by the Austro-German classics. But before the Nazis' accession to power he had nevertheless gladly performed the music of leading modernists. Thus he had given the world première of Schoenberg's dodecaphonic Variations for Orchestra op. 31 in 1928 and had conducted the more "extreme" works of Stravinsky (such as *Le sacre*), Bartók (his First Piano Concerto) and others. Such works disappeared from his concert programs in 1933, but they made no return to his repertoire after the end of the Third Reich. Instead, Furtwängler's programming was as conservative as ever, with just the occasional performance of Stravinsky's *Petrushka* or his Symphony in Three Movements amidst a sea of Wagner, Mendelssohn, Beethoven, Brahms, Bruckner, and Furtwängler (for he several times performed his own Second Symphony and Piano Concerto).[32] If Furtwängler needed a perceived enemy in order to be able to continue to compose, then the musical progressives were the only "natural" opponent left to him. He now began to speak and write of them as his outright adversaries, and he clearly saw his own oeuvre as a last bastion of defense against their supposed cultural barbarism. This could in turn explain his astonishing comparison of the atonal composers with Goebbels, for seen in this light it was a comparison divorced of any political aspect and instead purely personal in nature: Furtwängler needed them to appear alike if the former were to offer him a source of creative friction similar to that once furnished by the latter. This constant interplay of rejection and acceptance, discord and concord seems to Furtwängler to have been the inhaling and exhaling of his creative spirit. Sometimes, it seems, the muse will only descend when she is given battles to fight, be they ever so spurious.

CHAPTER FIVE

HERE COMES
THE SUNSET

The Late and the
Last Works of Richard Strauss

L ateness was the saving grace of Richard Strauss. With a dash of hyperbole one might even say it saved him from a fate "worse" than death,
for it allowed him to avoid a postmortem reception history dominated by
moral revulsion. Posterity has not always been kind to Strauss but it would
have been a lot less so had he died, say, in 1934 when still president of the
Reichsmusikkammer, or in the early 1940s when courting the Nazi func-
tionaries Hans Frank and Baldur von Schirach while his son's Jewish in-
laws, the von Grabes, were being slaughtered in the death camps. After the
end of the Second World War, Strauss reinvented himself, and his muse enjoyed a remarkable late flowering. He found a new publisher, new friends,
new financial backers, and new markets while establishing, consciously or
not, a satisfying aesthetic narrative for his oeuvre that served to underpin
his rehabilitation.

This late burst of inspiration, his "Indian summer" as it is often termed,
was soon seen by most commentators as an act of rejuvenation, a return
to the innocent springs of youth. *Capriccio*, for some his operatic masterpiece,[1] was followed by the *Metamorphosen*, three concertos, and works
for wind ensemble. The narrative of his life closes with his "ultimate opus
ultimum,"[2] the *Four Last Songs*, whose apparent yea-saying acceptance of
his approaching end gives them the unusual status of a work supposedly
inspired by their composer's acceptance of his own approaching death.

Willi Schuh was one of the first to draw parallels between the early and the late Strauss, writing in *Tempo* as early as December 1945 that "since *Capriccio* Strauss has written only smaller instrumental works of a classicism which points back to his beginnings sixty-five years ago."[3] Just about everyone since has followed his lead. Bryan Gilliam has remarked in the *New Grove* on how Strauss returned "to the classic genres of his youth" after *Capriccio*.[4] And Michael Kennedy, in an article tellingly entitled "Strauss's Autumn Glory," has written how in these late works "the wheel came full circle from youth to old age. . . . He brought down the curtain on his eighty years of composing with songs which, for all the melancholy with which they are imbued, look back elatedly on 'a life full of thankfulness.' Tragedy darkened Strauss's last years, but in the works of his Indian Summer . . . the radiance of youth was still reflected in the mellowness of age."[5] Similar comments are to be found throughout the literature.[6]

To a certain degree this rings true. If we look at the Strauss work catalogue, we indeed find similarities between the early and the late. His early works include a horn concerto, a violin concerto, and a *Burleske* for piano and orchestra, plus solo pieces with orchestra for cello and for clarinet. This fascination with concertante works returns in his last years with the composition of concertos for horn, oboe, and a clarinet-bassoon duo. The dances arranged from *Capriccio* were his first music for piano trio since his teenage years, and his late sonatinas for sixteen winds harken back to the early Suite and Serenade, each for thirteen winds, written sixty years earlier. But these comparisons must be treated with caution. For there are concertante works from Strauss's middle years as well (the *Parergon* of 1925 and the *Panathenäenzug* of 1927), just as there are works for wind and brass from the same time (his two fanfares of 1924). He composed many piano works in his early years, none in the late (unless one counts the brief harpsichord dances taken from *Capriccio*). And there is nothing in Strauss's final decade along the lines of his two early symphonies or his other early, abstract orchestral works. Concertos aside, his late works for orchestra, from his unfinished symphonic poem *The Danube* to the *Metamorphosen*, show that program music in its various guises still fascinated him. So to talk of Strauss returning as an old man to the genres of his youth—in his end is his beginning—must be properly contextualized, as it offers a sense of rounding off to his career that is as much in the minds of his commentators as in the music itself.

Nevertheless, were it not for certain undeniable aspects of his biography and his oeuvre, this notion of Strauss coming full circle would not have proven so durable. In the 1940s he was increasingly concerned with ensuring his place in history, which inevitably prompted retrospection, both musical and otherwise. The early years of the decade saw him putting various reminiscences to paper, as with "Erinnerungen an meinen Vater" (Reminiscences of my father) and "Aus meinen Jugend- und Lehrjahren" (From the years of my youth and studies). The first sentence of the former article offers a prime example of the aging composer's desire to record history as he wanted it to be known. He states that his father's father had been a town watchman, though it is a lie, for the town watchman was his father's uncle: Franz Strauss was an illegitimate child who never really knew his own father.[7] But an aging composer keen to impress upon posterity his legitimate rights of inheritance within the Austro-German tradition could hardly admit to any such proximity to bastardy. Strauss's other articles and letters of the same decade might not be quite as blasé in their attitude to historical truth, but they leave no doubt of Strauss's determination to occupy a preeminent place in music history, nor of his conviction that his works would dominate the German stages, concert halls, and radio waves of the future. Even on April 27, 1945, just days before the end of the war, he wrote to Karl Böhm in all seriousness to outline his vision of the coming music life of Vienna, despite the city and its institutions having been reduced to rubble. He stipulated all kinds of detail, even down to how many first and second violins should be engaged in the (as yet nonexistent) opera houses. And he gave precise repertoire lists that included all his own works, but which expressly banned "from the German stage" Rossini's *Guillaume Tell* and Verdi's *Otello* and *Don Carlos*—as if Germany had not had enough proscriptions over the previous twelve years.[8] Given that there was at this time almost no music life anywhere in greater Germany, all this was either a hopeless mixture of arrogance and denial—which would fit the accepted picture of Strauss at the end of the war as a tired, grumpy old man no longer willing or able to acknowledge the horrors perpetrated in the name of his fatherland—or it was a sign of remarkable percipience. In the end he was largely proven right. The German opera houses were indeed rebuilt, and *Salome* and *Rosenkavalier* became big earners once again, just as his orchestral works have since become preeminent in the recording market.

Strauss had occasionally made miscalculations in his affairs, such as the large investments in England that were lost as a result of the First World War or his later conviction that the Nazis would not dare interfere in his choice of librettist, even if he chose a Jew such as Stefan Zweig. But seen as a whole, Strauss's decades-long endeavors to ensure the financial and social status of his family were marked by continual success. Despite having a Jewish daughter-in-law and half-Jewish grandchildren, he had managed to ally himself with Nazis (such as Baldur von Schirach and Hans Frank)

prominent enough to offer protection during the Holocaust, and he succeeded in having his grandsons declared "honorary Aryans" on the order
of the *Führer*.[9] In the last years of the war, he was increasingly concerned
that his music should survive and prosper, and he understood, too, that a
proper telling of his life was intrinsic to the long-term success of the project.
Thus in December 1941 he tasked Willi Schuh with writing his biography.
His choice was astute: Schuh had a reputation for thoroughness mixed with
a certain dry objectivity; he was German-speaking, but his nationality was
that of neutral Switzerland (handy, depending on how the war progressed);
and he was a great admirer of Strauss (as a nineteen-year-old student just
after the First World War, Schuh had travelled for some two days by train to
attend the world premiere of Strauss's *Frau ohne Schatten* in Vienna—a sure
sign of devotion if ever there were one).[10] The biography was just one aspect
of Strauss's wider concern to consolidate his achievements. In September
1942 he began planning an edition of his correspondence with his parents;
in 1943 he was impressing on his son the importance of organizing a proper
work catalogue and a complete edition of his songs; and in May 1944 he was
planning a "Strauss Verlag" to publish his works—an idea realized some fifty
years later. His plans to found a "Richard Strauss Archive" in Vienna in July
1944 under the auspices of Baldur von Schirach were unsuccessful at the
time, but came to fruition half a century later in Garmisch.

Fluctuating health and the uncertain state of life in postwar Germany
prompted Strauss to move to Switzerland in October 1945. There he was
confident that old friends and colleagues would treat him with the defer-
ence he felt he was owed, and he could be assured of any medical attention he and his wife might need. Problems at Bregenz on the border were
easily solved. Strauss had deposited numerous manuscripts there during
the war and wished to take them with him into Switzerland. The Prince
of Saxony, an old acquaintance, was resident in Bregenz and intervened
to help negotiate with the French occupying authorities. The French com-
mandant was given the manuscript of one of Strauss's Weinheber songs,
op. 88, as was one of the French majors. A lieutenant was given a page of
sketch, and the score of the *Alpine Symphony* was presented for donation
to the Bibliothèque Nationale in Paris. Strauss had long realized the material value of his scores and was perfectly capable of de facto bribery if the
end result was desirable. The Strausses crossed the border with no further
problems. Strauss now called upon the services of Maria Jeritza, the wife
of the wealthy American businessman Irving Seery, to help him sell manuscript copies of earlier works that he had been preparing for purely money-
making purposes.

Strauss and Pauline spent almost four years in Switzerland. They were not without initial money worries, as his royalties were frozen, but still they managed to live in the same luxurious hotels they had frequented in the years when money had flowed freely. Willi Schuh placed his own network of contacts at Strauss's disposal. The rich patrons Paul Sacher and Werner Reinhart ensured that the composer received new performances. And Boosey and Hawkes, who during the war had bought up the rights to much of Strauss's music from his exiled publisher Fürstner, now dispatched Ernst Roth, assistant to Ralph Hawkes, to negotiate the publication of Strauss's newest works. The opera houses of Zurich, Basle, and Berne feted him as ever they had, and acquaintances old and new provided the comfort and the liquid assets needed to fund a comfortable lifestyle. First and foremost among these was Adolf Jöhr, the Germanophile, millionaire director of the Credit Suisse bank who had enjoyed close business connections with Nazi Germany and even closer family connections to Swiss fascism (Jöhr's son, Walter Adolf, was a prominent Swiss fascist in the 1930s who also wrote pro-fascist tracts such as *America und der Faschismus*).[11] Strauss was also lucky that the former Swiss general consul in Munich from 1942 to 1944, the music-loving Hans Zurlinden, was from 1945 to 1946 stationed back in Berne. They had become well acquainted during the war, with Zurlinden attending the world premiere of *Capriccio* in 1942 and being invited on occasion to Garmisch. Strauss now called upon him for everyday matters, such as sending parcels of chocolate and the like to his son Franz and daughter-in-law Alice back home, and also for political tasks such as arranging a meeting with the Swiss Federal President Eduard von Steiger. This Zurlinden did in November 1945.[12] There were champagne evenings with the *haute bourgeoisie*, teatimes with conservatory directors, dinners with politicians, car jaunts with businessmen, and get-togethers with other leading artists, such as Wilhelm Furtwängler and Wilhelm Backhaus, who had also found their way across the border. While we should not underestimate the psychological impact of leaving home and family behind at an age of over eighty, Strauss's voluntary exile was eminently successful.

Strauss had remained active at the end of the war, writing the *Metamorphosen* for Paul Sacher, plus uncommissioned new works and arrangements of older ones that allowed him to arrive in Switzerland with enough novelties to keep him in the public eye. There was an oboe concerto, a new sonatina for sixteen wind instruments, and a new version of his waltz "Munich," and these were joined by a symphonic fantasy based on the *Frau ohne Schatten*, a "symphonic fragment" from the

Josephs Legende, and a new arrangement of the *Rosenkavalier* waltzes (Strauss always knew what sold best). According to Adolf Jöhr's reminiscences, Boosey & Hawkes paid him the enormous sum of 50,000 Swiss Francs for these waltzes (for purposes of comparison, Othmar Schoeck, the leading Swiss German composer of his day, was at this time paid 1,000 Swiss Francs by his Swiss publisher for a cello concerto of a half-hour's duration). Strauss's check was held up by the Allied authorities, but when Jöhr intervened and brought to the attention of the French financial attaché Strauss's donation to France of the *Alpine Symphony*, the money was released.[13]

Strauss's de-Nazification proceeded smoothly, and in January 1947 he was made a citizen of Austria, an officially "liberated" country. But Strauss's efforts to restore his reputation after the war and achieve rehabilitation seem to have been largely focused on the English-speaking world. An invitation to Hollywood from the actor Lionel Barrymore came to nothing on account of the negative press that Strauss was getting in America at the time.[14] In England, things went better. *Tempo* in particular devoted numerous articles to him from 1944 onward, with Willi Schuh prominent among their authors. Beginning with extracts in English from Stefan Zweig's autobiography in June 1944, *Tempo* slowly but surely began to paint a favorable picture of Strauss's involvement in German cultural affairs under the Nazis. In December 1945, Schuh broached the topic directly with "Strauss during the War Years" in *Tempo*,[15] in which he set the tone for his articles of the ensuing years with a portrayal of a composer who is essentially without sin, since he inhabits a "spiritual domain" that "the affairs of the world of to-day do not enter."[16] For *Tempo* to invest so much ink and space on Richard Strauss made perfect sense. The journal was run by Boosey & Hawkes, and Ernst Roth was presumably keen to promote his company's newest and potentially most profitable acquisition. Most of all, Strauss had to be absolved of any political unsoundness that could be bad for business. The culmination of Strauss's rehabilitation in the West was a three-week journey to England in October 1947 to attend a Strauss Festival organized by Roth and Thomas Beecham. Strauss sat in the royal box in the Theater Royal, conducted "God Save the King" and works of his own in the Royal Albert Hall, sauntered through galleries, and ate in the Athenaeum Club. He stayed at the Savoy and dined on oysters and champagne, though the press and his handlers so outdid themselves in the art of spin that the reading public came to believe that Strauss had been plunged into near-poverty. One woman even sent ten shillings out of pity for him, obviously unaware that his new arrangement of the *Rosenkavalier Waltzes* alone was bringing him over five thousand times as much.[17] Two years later, just weeks before Strauss's death in the summer of 1949, *Tempo* even issued a celebratory "Richard Strauss Number"—a significant turnabout for a former President of the *Reichsmusikkammer* just four years after the cessation of hostilities.

There were ups and downs, early glitches in his liquidity, bouts of depression, and health problems unsurprising for a man in his early eighties emerging from six years in a war-ravaged country. Yet little seems to have changed about Strauss. The general picture offered in the literature is of a tired old man tossed about by fate, the last representative of an outdated aesthetic, compelled to let things take their course yet finally approaching his own end with equanimity. This has been convincing and convenient, partly because it plays on our natural sympathy for the aged and infirm, but also because it arguably allows us to extend the supposed passivity of the octogenarian composer back into the 1930s. This in turn implicitly exonerates him from any conscious collaboration with the Nazi regime. But his music offers a different interpretation of the late Strauss. Commentators have long been at one in judging his late works, from *Capriccio* to the *Four Last Songs*, as having returned (with one or two exceptions) to the aesthetic heights of his earlier work after the dull banalities of *Friedenstag* and *Die Liebe der Danäe*. As a conductor, too, his mental and physical stamina remained impressive. When he conducted a full program comprising *Don Juan*, the *Burleske*, and the *Symphonia Domestica* in London in 1947, the critic of the *Times* remarked, "How exact that beat is! How infinite the gradation of expression conveyed by variations in the movement of the stick! At eighty-three his command of the orchestra and his ability to obtain from it exactly what he wants remain undiminished."[18] If his mind was capable of creating the inspired complexities of his late scores, and if he was physically and mentally fit enough to conduct a vast orchestra in a two-hour symphonic program (standing up to do so, as the sources confirm), then it seems highly unlikely that Strauss should have become muddled or semisenile whenever his mind turned to business or politics.

Adolf Jöhr's reminiscences of Strauss in 1947 and 1948 depict a man in full control of his faculties, cognizant of his market value, knowing when to act swiftly for immediate gain—such as using manuscripts as collateral or writing new arrangements of old works—and when to hold out for greater, later profits, as in his determination not to give the world premiere of his *Liebe der Danäe* to a "provincial" Swiss opera house, but to wait for the rebuilding of first-rate ensembles across the border in Germany.[19] All the biographical facts confirm that Strauss remained a cunning player, still adept at courting the wealthy, the powerful, and the titled and at placing himself at the center of attention. He did not even shy away from suggesting seriously in a letter of February 20, 1947, that Ernst Roth should contact the Foreign Office in London or Bevin or Churchill directly in order to procure Swiss visas for his son and grandchildren. They ought to be allowed to see their "famous" father and grandfather again "before his death," he wrote, obviously convinced that a spot of emotional blackmail in high places would do the trick.[20] No passive actor he, but an active agent possessed of a steely determination to reinvent himself for a successful career in a postwar world while somehow convincing those around him (and us in turn) of his innocence and passivity in the face of approaching death. The uncomfortable questions regarding his collaboration during the Nazi period are better contextualized if we admit that he had always been and always remained a "collaborator," though the word is admittedly loaded. Whether as music director of the Kaiser's Court Opera, Director of the post–First World War Vienna State Opera, President of the *Reichsmusikkammer*, or as the "penniless exile" in Switzerland, Strauss had never failed to play the role that those in power had expected of him in exchange for quality of life. He wrote marches for the Kaiser, a national anthem for the Austrian Republic (albeit never officially adopted), an "Olympic Hymn" for Hitler's Games—and he conducted "God Save the King" in London. The men to whom Strauss felt closest in the Third Reich were also those who swayed whichever way the wind blew, first among them Clemens Krauss and Karl Böhm. Nor should we be surprised that he wrote his post-Zweig operas with collaborators: *Daphne*, *Friedenstag*, and *Die Liebe der Danäe* with Joseph Gregor, and *Capriccio* with Clemens Krauss.[21] The moment any man took a principled stand that went against his immediate self-interest—as in the case of Stefan Zweig's refusal to continue working as his librettist—Strauss seemed genuinely unable to comprehend him. The only "nation" that Strauss ever really acknowledged was the empire of music, the one in which, to his own mind, he had always occupied high offices of state. To him, his actions were not collaboration but merely giving unto Caesar what was Caesar's. In this he never hesitated, caring not a whit whether Caesar's name was Wilhelm, Adolf, or Winston. One of the few to remark on this was the young Friedelind Wagner, who wrote in her memoirs that "Strauss was a weather-vane, veering with every political wind. Monarchist, Social Democrat, a little pink, a little brown, he got along with all regimes."[22] When Willi Schuh brought this phrase to Strauss's attention, Strauss threatened legal action for libel, so it was removed from the German-language edition that was being prepared at the time. Strauss was truly a Teflon man, but no one was supposed to know it.

If this postwar Strauss was not a mere shadow of his younger self, as is sometimes supposed, then we should bear this in mind when considering those backward glances that we find in the music of his final decade. Consider *Capriccio*, as a prime example. The many self-quotations in which Strauss here indulges have been well documented. Italian singers perform set pieces just like the Italian tenor in *Der Rosenkavalier*; the "Mondschein-Musik" before the final scene is an elaboration of a theme Strauss took from his song cycle *Krämerspiegel*, op. 66, and the Countess has more than a touch of the Marschallin about her. And there is self-quotation as at the opening of the opera, in which the offstage music is identical to that of the prelude we have just heard played in the orchestra pit—being in a sense an echo or a "mirror" of it, just as the set itself (thus the stage directions) is full of mirrors on the walls. It is to one of these mirrors that the Countess speaks in her final scene, gazing contentedly and admiringly at herself after all the other characters have departed (although the cast list included a composer, Flamand, it seems likely that Strauss himself identified most with the Countess). Since *Capriccio* was written in 1940/41, it is tempting to see it as a flight from an unpalatable reality into the rarefied world of aesthetics, with Strauss the last man standing of the heirs to the Holy Flame of German art, admiring himself in the metaphorical mirror of his youth. But his inward gaze and his supposed ignorance of the horrors around him must have involved an element of choice. For had he really been so ignorant of the consequences of being Jewish in Nazi Germany, for example, he would not have been so keen to have his grandsons "Aryanized." Indeed, all the self-references and the mirrors in *Capriccio* seem to function as a kind of prison whose intent is more to keep the (real) world out than to keep anyone or anything in. This conscious rejection of the "outside" is here allied to Strauss's reluctance to entertain any notion of closure. Just as the instrumental prelude does not really end, but resumes offstage, so the end of the opera is no ending at all, but an unanswered question posed by the Countess to her reflection in the mirror, asking precisely what the "ending" might be. There is one character who does demand an effective exit, namely the aging theater director, but in an intentionally ironic twist, Strauss denies him one, having him leave the stage for the last time in a fadeout, instead.

Strauss's other late works are no less self-referential, as was remarked upon by his contemporaries. The critic of the *Musical Times* who reviewed the first London performance of the Oboe Concerto in 1946 wrote that it was "full of phrases that have a curious and agreeable twist in them, and of quick, far-away modulations like those in the first half-dozen bars of

Rosenkavalier. The ear caught many little half-echoes from that work, not as things recognized but rather as reminders of a familiar voice and turn of speech."[23] Strauss's fondness for quoting was not restricted to self-pilfering, for he further drew on the music of the Austro-German canon to which his own oeuvre belonged—also, no doubt, as an act of insistent confirmation of that same belonging (let us not forget his desire to affirm his aesthetic legitimacy). The most obvious example is the quotation from the funeral march of Beethoven's *Eroica* in his *Metamorphosen*. But the Oboe Concerto offers another, for its beginning is virtually a paraphrase of the opening of Mozart's overture to *The Marriage of Figaro*, in which the opening quavers and subsequent pause are retained but inverted, and in which the theme from measure 8 is given in slightly elaborated form, divided between orchestra and oboe solo (though at pitch, and at an approximation of the original rhythm). There is no recording of Strauss conducting the overture to *The Marriage of Figaro*, nor has his marked score survived,[24] though the tempo of Strauss's semiquavers clearly corresponds to that of Mozart's quavers (see exx. 5.1 and 5.2).

Strauss was hardly the first or the last composer to draw on works from his youth in old age, either in order to assure himself of his place in history, or in an attempt to refind inspiration that had been lacking in his more recent music. And his late retreat—it is difficult to avoid such loaded words—into the genres of his youth, his concertos and wind sonatinas, is in part precisely what we assume it to be: old age looking wistfully at earlier times, a fulfillment of the cliché we all feel must be true, that those who comb gray hair must yearn for the vigor of youth. It is strangely comforting to imagine the octogenarian Strauss rounding off a long career by returning to where he had once been before. It offers his biography an intrinsically musical form of closure—a kind of sonata form with inverted recapitulation where the first subject reappears reassuringly at the end in the tonic. But as we have seen with *Capriccio*, Strauss himself was at this time not as keen on closure as we might like to think. The coupling of youth and old age in the reception of his works was in his own interest, for it implicitly and conveniently ignored the years in between—the years, in other words, of Strauss's collaboration with the Nazis. It might be an act of overinterpretation to suggest that this was a conscious strategy, but it cannot be denied that these works of his last years succeeded in returning an aura of innocence to his biography that served to cancel out for many his association with the Butcher of Poland and his cohorts.

Of all his late works, it is primarily Strauss's *Four Last Songs*, three settings of Hermann Hesse and one of Joseph von Eichendorff

Example 5.1. Strauss, Oboe Concerto (1945), opening of the first movement, mm. 1–8. © Hawkes & Son (London), Ltd. Reproduced with permission.

completed in late 1948, that have seen "lateness" as the prime determinant in their reception history, as a brief selection of comments from some fifty years can confirm: they are his "swan song," his "final farewell," "on internal evidence alone . . . a deliberate valedictory offering for the various friends to whom they are inscribed and for the composer's admirers in general," "each a masterpiece . . . [that] brought down the curtain on his eighty years of composing," "a conscious farewell to the cherished beauties of the world," a work in which "he has come to his last moments and makes his farewell."[25] There is no denying the valedictory nature of the poems that Strauss set. In Hesse's "September," "The garden is in mourning . . . summer yearns for rest. Slowly he closes his tired eyes," while in "Beim Schlafengehen" (Going to sleep), the narrator wishes to "receive the starry night like a weary child . . . all my senses wish to sink into slumber. And

Example 5.2. Mozart, opening of the overture to *The Marriage of Figaro*, K. 492, mm. 1–14.

[my] unguarded soul will soar up freely . . . to live deeply and a thousand-fold." In this context, even the text of Hesse's "Im Frühling" (In the spring) seems to speak more of things past than of any present or future.

The last of the *Last*, "Im Abendrot" (In the sunset), a setting of a poem by Joseph von Eichendorff, implicitly takes up the topic of the previous song ("Beim Schlafengehen") with its setting free of the soul, but more obviously takes sleep as a metaphor for death. It is the one of the *Four* in which the "mood of leave-taking prevails most decisively."[26] It is also the most poignant, being not just a "farewell," but seemingly one to (and for) the composer's wife, as has been observed repeatedly since the songs were first published.[27] The poem addresses the narrator's partner as they wander "hand in hand" toward the sunset with two larks soaring above them. "Soon it will be time to sleep," he says, then asks: "Is this perhaps death?" No interpretation has ever seemed possible except the one in which it is Richard and Pauline who glide happily into the dusk. Unlike in *Capriccio*, Strauss here does not leave that final question unanswered. As Willi Schuh wrote in *Tempo* in advance of the world premiere of the songs in May 1950, "the autobiographical character emerges with especial distinctness in the concluding verse, where twice the horn solemnly sounds the transfiguration

theme from Strauss's Tone Poem *Death and Transfiguration*."[28] This quotation, heard as the two larks in the poem soar up to heaven, comes across
as an affirmative act of acceptance of an ineludible end, yet an end that is
somehow also a crossing-over to a new beginning. The stance of Strauss
the man seemed to confirm the message of Strauss the composer. When
asked by a journalist from *Life* magazine in 1947 of his plans for the future,
he replied: "Na, sterben halt"—"to die, of course."[29] If a Great Man can be
so stoic and content, if he can so happily refuse to rage against the dying of
the light, it is somehow comforting to the rest of us. It did not occur to the
journalist that Strauss was probably being sarcastic.

In fact, Strauss had already put death behind him. He had ceased assigning opus numbers to his music after op. 88 (his Weinheber songs of 1942)
and declared all subsequent works to be "posthumous." He further termed
them "wrist exercises" of primarily private interest.[30] But Strauss did nothing
to prevent these ostensibly private works from being performed publicly—
he promoted them as he always had promoted his music—and he personally
supervised the contracts for their later publication with Boosey & Hawkes.
All the same, a composer writing "posthumous" works must by definition
already have "died," and a "dead" composer has no more need to fear death.
This intellectual sleight of hand might seem a little absurd, and will not have
relieved Strauss of all concerns for the future, but it does seem to have helped
to free his mind and would appear to have contributed to the considerable
productivity of his last years. And Strauss's insistence that his late works were
of minor import (a claim contradicted by his actions on their behalf) has in
retrospect served merely to emphasize the image of him as a sympathetic old
man who at the end attained a transcendent modesty while continuing to
compose his works of genius.

The *Four Last Songs* were themselves also a sleight of hand, but this time
on the part of Strauss's publisher Ernst Roth, who (presumably together with
Willi Schuh) gave them their title and their present order. Their dedications,
however, were Strauss's own doing, and it is noteworthy that they are dedicated to the four personalities to whom Strauss owed his current liquidity
and his hopes for future income: Willi Schuh, Adolf Jöhr, Ernst Roth, and
Maria Jeritza. Strauss tactfully included the spouses of his sponsors (except
for Roth) in the dedications, for he was indirectly dependent upon them, too.
But as we well know, Strauss did not just write four; there was also "Malven,"
which he gave to Maria Jeritza and never orchestrated, and then there was
an orchestral version of the early "Ruhe meine Seele" that Tim Jackson has
argued belongs together with the new songs written in 1948.[31] So there
were never "four" *Last Songs*, nor is there any reason to believe that Strauss

intended them to be his last. Roth's role in the "mystification" of the songs has not gone unnoticed,[32] though his ordering proved so successful that critics right from the start found it difficult to believe that Strauss had not intended them thus. It was no secret that "Im Abendrot" had been the first of the *Four* to be written (sketches for it date from at least early 1947), though Alan Frank in *Music and Letters* echoed the general opinion at the time that it was "clearly intended as the last of the group."[33]

"Im Abendrot" is worth a closer look. There is indeed something deeply satisfying about its final position in the "cycle"; its sunset imagery and its closing question-and-answer make it a perfect swan song. But sunsets can be uncomfortable things. In his poem "The Baler" in *Human Chain*, Seamus Heaney recalls a visit from a friend not far from death who "could bear no longer to watch / The sun going down" and so asked "to be put / With his back to the window."[34] In a review of Heaney's collection in the *Independent*, Tom Sutcliffe recalled reading of a "Japanese architectural firm who had been commissioned to build a house for an elderly man. . . . His brief was for a modest building, with the added proviso that it should not have a view of the sunset, since he disliked its unavoidable symbolism."[35]

Perhaps only those who feel convinced that their own sunset lies far, far ahead can postulate a quiet contemplation of it. Strauss's sunset was right ahead of him and he knew it. If we want to believe that he was not scared of it, then this says more about us than about him. The idea that Strauss (a confirmed atheist) was waiting quietly for the darkness to envelop him and that he wanted to express this in his music is neither in keeping with what we know of the man's biography, nor what the music seems to be telling us. "Im Abendrot" is different from the other three of the "Last Four" not just in its poet, but also in its harmonic rhythm, which is often slow almost to the point of immobility. The music seems reluctant to leave the opening tonic, and at the end this same tonic is so insistent that it is as if we had never left it. Harmonic stasis is here surely a protest against teleology. If one never leaves home, then one need not fear reaching one's goal. A desire to be "home" is crucial to the song. The words "how we are tired of wandering" have usually been interpreted metaphorically as a longing to find a final resting place, whereas Strauss probably meant them quite literally. He wanted to return to his house in Garmisch, the place where he had always been most productive as a composer. And he presumably wanted to return to live and work, not just to die.

Then there is the matter of that final quotation from *Death and Transfiguration*, which is set off from the rest of the song as if it were in inverted commas. As Schuh himself pointed out, it is stated twice. Since there cannot be two separate transfigurations, one after the other (not if the narrator and partner are still hand in hand and doing everything together, simultaneously, living and dying and being transfigured), then we must assume that this duplication was for reasons of insistence. It also reinforces the impression one has of the theme being a foreign body, something derived from elsewhere (which indeed it is). It is as if the composer wanted to make sure we notice it, drawing our attention aggressively to its poignancy—like an infirm beggar displaying his wounds to passers-by in order to elicit increased sympathy. But a poignancy aware of itself, doubly hammered home, is in the end not so poignant any more. The composer is here playing with our imagined emotional response, doing just what the world expects of an aging composer—writing of death—while engaged in an act of subversion against us, determined to tell us what we are allowed to feel. It is not so far removed from the emotional blackmail that he practiced in his personal dealings, as in the letter to Roth mentioned earlier. It is a blackmail that has worked on most conductors, for the tempi generally favored for this song are so morbidly labored that one is sometimes surprised the singer does not herself expire before the end. The extant recordings that Strauss made of *Death and Transfiguration* have a tempo of about ♩ = 66–70 for the "big tune" at the end, and since Strauss the conductor was remarkably consistent in his tempi throughout his career,[36] we must assume that he had this tempo in his mind when he wrote "Im Abendrot." With the exception of Georg Solti, however (a conductor who met Strauss in his final years and observed him closely on the rostrum), most conductors have taken the song slowly and its end even slower, at about ♩ = 40.[37]

This repetition of that "transfiguration" theme, however, might not have been intended merely for Strauss's listeners, but could also have been of personal significance. In an article entitled "Vom melodischen Einfall" (On melodic inspiration) of ca. 1940, he had written as follows:

> Such "Einfälle" very often arrive in the morning when one awakes, thus in that moment when the brain, emptied of blood during the night, is filled again with fresh blood. . . . What is an Einfall? In general we call a musical Einfall a motive, a melody, that suddenly "occurs" to me, uncalled by the intellect, especially in the morning immediately after waking up, or in a dream. . . . My own experience is this: If I get stuck somewhere while composing on an evening . . . I go to sleep, and in the morning when I awake *the continuation is there.*[38]

We can ignore Strauss's odd sanguinary musings, for what is significant is how he follows the lead of Wagner in situating the moment of inspiration in the boundary between sleeping and waking. As elucidated in our opening chapter, Wagner had developed this notion under the influence of Schopenhauer's "Über das Geistersehen" and elaborated it in his essay on Beethoven in 1870. (While Wagner was not the first artist to stress the importance of semiconsciousness in his inspiration, as we have also noted variously above, he was in most things Strauss's first point of reference, and he was presumably in this case, too).[39]

In *Death and Transfiguration*, the "big tune" at the close signifies not only the "transfiguration" of the dying artist but also the concept of the *Einfall* as Strauss understood it, that moment of inspiration experienced in the intermediary realm just beyond consciousness. This could offer us a further reason for Strauss's repetition of the theme in "Im Abendrot." His health was failing and he had recently had to submit to unpleasant irrigations of the bladder. He also knew he had to keep on composing to ensure the benevolence of those around him until he could access all his royalties and finally be able to return home. This quotation thus becomes an act of snatching inspiration from the jaws of oblivion, reversing the narrator's drift into the beyond: for in Strauss's aesthetic, the *Einfall* experienced in that borderline state is a signal that triggers the mind back into awareness. By taking as its close a passage that Strauss had written nearly sixty years before, "Im Abendrot" in fact finishes, in chronological terms, "before" it has even begun, in yet another rejection of the end of life. This double quotation of the *Einfall* from his early symphonic poem thus serves as a kind of repeated, shamanic summoning of the creative powers of his youth as a means of rejuvenating his muse. It worked, for within some four months of completing this song in April 1948, Strauss had written and scored three others. In just eight months more, he returned home to Garmisch. Nor let us forget that the song is "*Im* Abendrot"—"In the sunset," not after it. It holds the setting sun firmly in its metaphorical grasp, not letting it sink out of sight, just as the two twittering larks soar up and up, implicitly remaining illumined by its rays—for as the sun sinks, so they rise. Furthermore: if, as all commentators have assumed, Strauss indeed intended the song as a portrait of himself and Pauline, then by assigning the vocal part to a soprano, it is "she" who poses the final question about death, allowing him to confront it at a remove.

If we pause to consider again the stock interpretation of the *Four Last Songs*, mentioned in the opening paragraph, in which Strauss was inspired to great art by the prospect of his own death—by the prospect, in other words, of his imminent incapacity to be inspired by anything—then the absurdity of that interpretation becomes apparent. The *Four Last Songs* were not inspired by death, nor do they offer any quiet acceptance of it. Rather are they an act of defiance in the face of it, and they confirm Strauss's undiminished desire to assure his music's place in history and its proceeds in his bank account. It is Strauss's ability and willingness to compose *about* death that is his very proof of life. Naming death (the poem's final word)—regardless of whether it is "his" voice or "Pauline's" that utters it—helps him to tame his fears, to believe for a moment that he can control it, even if he knows objectively that he cannot. Strauss's late works offer no sentimental, backward glance at youth, nor a serene acceptance of an inevitable end. Rather, they are they the product of a fecund creative mind affirming its continuing existence. Even when he seems to be saying farewell, Strauss is glorying in the vitality of the present. And his music has no less to say to us on account of it.

POSTLUDE

The Telephone Call

In an interview for the *Paris Review*, the writer Anthony Burgess once remarked: "I can't understand the American literary block—as in Ellison or Salinger—unless it means that the blocked man isn't forced economically to write."[1] If a lack of economic necessity can prevent an artist from writing, then one might infer the reverse and suggest that an artist's "inspiration" can be prompted by the very prospect of money. This is contrary to the romantic image of an artist starving for his art in a garret and deriving his or her inspiration from adverse circumstances, an image that has always appealed more to the general public than it ever has to artists themselves (witness the example of Giacomo Puccini, whose romantic depiction of such starving, garret-bound artists in *La Bohème* was so successful financially that he never had to share their fate).

As we have seen in the case studies of this book, artists have often been keen to mythologize when talking about their work, preferring to leave monetary and social aspects out of the creative equation. It can be instructive here to compare two accounts from the same composer on the gestation of a specific work, one destined for posterity, the other not. When asked by Robert Craft what he meant by "the weight of an interval," Stravinsky answered:

> Let me tell you about a dream that came to me while I was composing *Threni*. After working late one night I retired to bed still troubled by an interval. I dreamed about this interval. It had become an elastic substance stretching exactly between the two notes I had composed, but underneath these notes at either end was an egg, a large testicular egg. The eggs were gelatinous to the touch (I touched them), and warm, and they were protected by nests. I woke up knowing that my interval was right. . . . Also, I was so surprised to see the eggs I immediately understood them

to be symbols. Still in the dream I went to my library of dictionaries and looked up "interval," but found only a confusing explanation which I checked the next morning in reality and found to be the same.[2]

The psychoanalytical import of Stravinsky's warm, viscous, testicular eggs is not what concerns us here, rather the fact that his inspiration receives confirmation from some deep, implicitly spiritual source, be it his subconscious or something beyond it. He told not dissimilar stories about the genesis of others of his works, most famously in the case of his *Rite of Spring*, of which he said: "I heard and I wrote what I heard. I am the vessel through which the *Sacre* passed."[3] Rolf Liebermann, who commissioned *Threni*, told a different story about that work's genesis, however:

> It was already 1956 or 57, I was here at the NDR [North German Radio] in Hamburg and came into the happy situation of being able to ask [Stravinsky] whether he might not want to write a piece for the NDR. We would be happy, we had everything he needed. I had been promised a sum of 10,000 dollars by the Intendant in Hamburg for the commission fee. That was a proper sum back then. He said: "Yes, I agree, I'll write the piece for you all." Then the next morning at seven o' clock I got a telephone call from our common friend [Nicolas] Nabokov, who said: "Stravinsky hasn't slept the whole night, he can't write the piece." I rang Stravinsky immediately and asked: "Maestro, what's wrong, why can't you write the piece?" He answered: "I can't do it for ten thousand dollars, I need eleven." I then rang Hamburg again and asked: "Can I spend eleven?" They laughed and said: "Yes, it's childish really, just accept eleven." That's how the piece came about.[4]

The two stories are by no means mutually exclusive, though the use of "I can't" in Liebermann's account rather than "I won't" or "I don't want to" (assuming that Liebermann is quoting the composer correctly) suggests that Stravinsky's ability to compose—his "inspiration," not his volition— was blocked by monetary considerations. One is reminded of the reply given by the songwriter Sammy Cahn when asked about the inspiration for his songs: whether the words or the music came first. It was neither, he said, but "the telephone call."[5]

One easily forgets that there are still artistic professions largely untouched by the apparent dichotomy between inspiration and volition that the romantics have bequeathed us. Anyone commissioning a carpenter to make a table would be surprised if he called after several months to explain that he had not yet felt inspired enough to begin it, just as a company organizing a competition to build a multimillion-dollar office block would be justifiably perplexed if one of the competing architects asked for an extension of the deadline until his muse descended. The utilitarian aspect of creating a building or a piece of furniture was not always absent from the world of music. As mentioned in the introduction, at precisely the time when aesthetic debates were raging between late romantics and modernists about the nature and significance of "inspiration," Arnold Schering published his article explaining that the *ars inveniendi*, the "art of invention" was until the later eighteenth century still something that one could learn, just as one learns harmony and counterpoint.[6] When composers began to write and talk of "inspiration" at the turn of the eighteenth and nineteenth centuries, music left the realm of artisanship, and composers, freed from the bonds of service to an employer (be it the church or an aristocrat), began working in a free market. In such a market, talent alone is rarely enough to ensure prosperity; as the word suggests, that talent must be marketed. It was not by chance that the early nineteenth century was the moment when composers began to pen prose as well as music, the former in order to explain and sell the latter to a bourgeoisie possessing increased access to the published word and keen to learn.

In the romantic era, the intangible nature of music made its claims to transcendence far more compelling than any that could be made for the other arts. This in turn made its inspiration "myths," several of which have been described and investigated in these pages, all the more attractive, even when they were conceived primarily as a marketing tool by the composer himself (as in Wagner's vision of La Spezia). These notions of transcendent inspiration, taken largely at face value, took hold of the Western imagination in a fashion not without consequence. As we have seen, Wagner's claims of the near-sainthood of the inspired composer helped his successors to insist on divorcing their art from those planes of human existence deemed less transcendent. Thus it was that Wilhelm Furtwängler was able to claim that his devotion to his art exonerated him of any guilt in the crimes perpetrated by the politicians whom he had served and who had paid his wages. Furtwängler was not alone. As discussed, a similar stance was adopted by post-1945 apologists for Richard Strauss.[7]

Such cases make it all the more pertinent to question the notions of inspiration that Wagner and his successors did so much to propagate. Yet while it is meet and right to reveal untruths where we find them, we should not ignore why such lies have so long proven so compelling. It is significant that Wagner's apologists, acolytes, and successors took his own stories of inspiration far more literally than he did himself. While it took over a hundred years to disprove some of his stories, such as that of La Spezia, he himself admitted to Cosima (as discussed in chapter 1 above) that his claim of having been inspired to *Parsifal* on and by Good Friday morning in 1857 was false. Or, rather: it was to him a poetic embellishment and reinterpretation that provided the conception of his creative ideas with a historically fixed time, place, and causality ("That's how it ought to be on Good Friday," he said).[8] What Wagner regarded as useful allegories were treated as incontrovertible facts by his successors (especially by those who desired to assume his mantle). Inspired by both Wagner and Schopenhauer (from whom Wagner had derived many of his views on the topic), several of them seem to have felt that aesthetic validity would best be attained by assigning a similar historical specificity and autobiographical justification to the nascence of their own musical ideas; treating his fictions as truths prompted them to create fictions of their own. Thus Mahler's lightning bolt at von Bülow's funeral or Berg's empathetic shock at the death of Manon Gropius. As we have seen in the case of Stravinsky, even composers who seemed keen to profess the objectivity of their art were not willing to jettison the myths of inspiration that they felt enhanced their status and helped to sell their wares.

It is natural for man to ponder the origins of his creativity, and since those origins lie in processes of the mind beyond immediate comprehension, a resort to fantasy in order to describe them should not surprise us. How better to describe the functioning of the imagination than with further flights of it? It may seem calculating for a composer to do so when, say, it entails "misusing" the death of another human being in order to promote his work all the better. But because the work of art is itself a coming-together of imagination and calculation, of inspiration and perspiration, we should not be shocked if a composer uses not dissimilar means—whether consciously or not—to describe to others the initial moment of composition and thus attempt to determine in advance the reception of his work.

As discussed in the introduction, the late-romantic composer Hans Pfitzner (1869–1949) was, if anything, even more obsessed with notions of quasi-divine inspiration than his contemporaries. This was not surprising, given that he saw himself as one of the prime aspirants to Wagner's mantle but was ever aware that few others felt him suited to the role. Never a man to use a shovel when a bulldozer would do, he became embroiled in aesthetic disputes with numerous perceived foes, from composers such as Ferruccio Busoni and Alban Berg to critics such as Paul Bekker. Pfitzner's final book, *Über musikalische Inspiration*, published in 1940, is a tract as angry and bitter as anything else he wrote, and in it he sums up the views on inspiration (often admittedly nebulous) that had already dominated his writings of the previous decades. He refers again to Wagner and to Schopenhauer and draws on Beethoven, Weber, Schumann, and Reger in order to underline his argument that inspiration—*Einfall*—is the mystery at the core of all good music, and that the aim of his critics and the modernists was to "rationalize" inspiration and thereby to deprive music of it.[9] He still saw contemporary music as a battle between the inspired heirs of Wagner in the Austro-German tradition (primarily himself) and those whose overintellectual, emotional aridity resulted in "musical impotence."

Pfitzner draws repeatedly on one specific work of his own to bolster his arguments: his opera *Palestrina*, whose first act offers a staged example of a dream-vision of musical inspiration. This scene is the most crucial in the work, and an operatic equivalent of Wagner's La Spezia vision or of Mahler's lightning bolt (though Pfitzner himself would probably have allowed comparison only with the former). The composer Palestrina is old and tired, and since the death of his wife, his muse has left him. The Council of Trent is debating a ban on polyphony; Cardinal Borromeo urges Palestrina in vain to write a new mass that will convince the Council and "save" the art of music. Palestrina is then visited in a vision by the ghosts of his long-dead predecessors, all urging him to write, and they are followed by a choir of angels who dictate to him what is to become his *Missa Papae Marcelli*. The fact that Palestrina is under economic, social, and political duress to compose is often overlooked (were this the real Palestrina, an eager musicologist might deconstruct his vision as a fiction intended to hide his acquiescence in the unjust political hierarchies of his day and would highlight the economic and social benefit that his mass brings him). But the dream-vision is striking both because it is a composed-out expression of an inspiration myth and also because its own level of "inspiration" is on a par with the moment of genius that it aims to depict. It is no wonder that the opera so fired the imagination of Pfitzner's contemporaries, foremost among them Thomas Mann.

For our purposes here, this scene in Pfitzner's *Palestrina* is of significance because we find corollaries to it in unexpected places. In an interview with Christopher Ballantine published in 1996, Joseph Shabalala of Ladysmith Black Mambazo recalled his musical education as follows:

> For a period of six months in 1964, [Shabalala] was visited in his dreams every night by a choir "from above" who sang to him. It was, he says, just like a nightly show—but he was the only listener. "I'm sleeping, but I'm watching the show. I saw myself sleeping but watching just like when you are watching TV."

"I was lucky to be trained by that spiritual group. These people were my teachers. I learnt everything about music from those people."

Initially, the people in this choir were invisible; Shabalala was able to "see" them only later. Even then he did not recognize any of them, and is still unable to say who there were. Very little was clear about them; not even whether they were black or white, female or male, young or old. With some hesitation, he calls them "children"—but only metaphorically, in the sense, as he puts it, that "they were children of God." They communicated not with their mouths, but "spirit to spirit." And they didn't speak; they only sang, and then in a strange language that Shabalala had not heard before. He believes this was deliberate, for what they wanted him to do was to concentrate on the harmony, the rhythm, and the experience, and then to think further. But while their words remained obscure, their music did not. He enjoyed it: "I felt like it was mine." And then the time came when he started to join them in their singing, every night.

Shabalala maintains that by visiting him in his dreams, the choir was responding to some worries he had had for a long time about the condition of Zulu music. In particular, as a talented and idealistic young man he had felt that the music had ceased to develop, or to develop in an appropriate manner. He had asked himself: "What's going on? This is wonderful, but where's the way?" The choir intervened. "I was a person who's looking for a way to develop our music, and this group of people was sent by somebody above to come and teach me."

A later dream assumed the significance of a final examination and graduation ceremony, giving him the confidence and authority to become the composer-leader of an *isicathamiya* group. He dreamt he was sitting on a revolving chair in the middle of a circle of 24 wise old men: "I used to call them the senior, the golden oldies, married men—the old ones with white hair." . . . Shabalala is unable to say who these elders were. I asked him if he would describe them as ancestors. "No, more than that! . . . They were the 24 who *trained* that choir!"[10]

We can be relatively sure that Pfitzner had no knowledge of such tales of dream-inspiration among peoples of other continents (his frame of reference being decidedly Wagnerian-Schopenhauerian), and we can be just as sure that Shabalala had no knowledge of Pfitzner's *Palestrina*. But regardless of how literally we wish to interpret Shabalala's dream, no caveats or doubts can alter the fact that the similarities between his account and Pfitzner's *Palestrina* are all the more striking for being independent of each other. In fact, there are similar, obviously independent tales of dream-inspiration in indigenous music cultures from the Canadian Atlantic coast to the jungles of Southeast Asia.[11] Just as there exist similar creation myths in different cultures across the world, so it seems that the act of musical creation has elicited independent but similar explanations unconnected by any form of causality.

This lack of causality and connection must give us pause for thought. We should not imagine that composers in non-Western traditions are less given to untruth or deception than are their Western counterparts, and we should note that stories of inspiration from the ancestors (just like Wagner's vision of La Spezia) may serve to enhance the status of the dreamer-composer among his peers. But the fact that musical inspiration is explained in similar fashion in communities of widely differing social, political, and economic structures, where the role of the composer can range from that of entertainer to sage and shaman, suggests that we should temper our revisionism when dealing with what might otherwise seem the self-serving products of fantasy of composers eager to gain a unique position for themselves in a busy marketplace.

As we have seen in our case studies, any discussion of musical inspiration that restricts itself to its "extraconscious," extrarational aspects— whether these be dreams, visions, "lightning bolts," moments of great emotion or phenomena beyond the ken of the composer or commentator—while ignoring other, more conscious determinants ranging from a composer's unavoidable acts of self-reflection on his art to issues of social acceptance and economic necessity will be misleading. But nor should we make the same mistake in reverse. For while the epiphanies discussed in these chapters may indeed encompass many lies and half-lies, were we to interpret musical creation as a primarily utilitarian act of economic and social self-empowerment, we would be both denying ourselves an aspect of reception that enriches our own experience of the music and ignoring the testimony (however factually flawed it may be) of the men and women who produce it. Acknowledging the one does not preclude appreciating the other, and we should also be prepared to regard apparent mendacities for a moment outside the realm of truth/untruth and to interpret them in the sense of Wagner's visions of La Spezia and Good Friday: as allegories that allow us alternative, symbolic points of access to an understanding of complex, barely understandable phenomena. If it is often the finest composers who have seemed most intent on determining a restricted view of the genesis of their works, then it is up to us to cast open the gates and allow for the multitude of meanings that they, their work, and we deserve.

NOTES

Introduction

Epigraph: Schoenberg, *"Stile herrschen, Gedanken siegen,"* 134. This and all translations in this volume are by the author unless stated otherwise.

1. See Schoenberg, "Inspiration," in *"Stile herrschen, Gedanken siegen,"* 134. See also in this regard the discussion of the "lightning bolt" of inspiration in chapter 2 of this book.

2. Voss, *Die Entstehung von Thomas Manns Roman "Doktor Faustus,"* 180.

3. Friedrich von Hausegger, "Aus dem Jenseits des Künstlers," 372–76.

4. Pfitzner, *Die neue Aesthetik,* 24.

5. Pfitzner, *Die neue Aesthetik,* 25.

6. Pfitzner, *Die neue Aesthetik,* 59.

7. Pfitzner, *Die neue Aesthetik,* 62.

8. Pfitzner, *Die neue Aesthetik,* 109.

9. Pfitzner, *Die neue Aesthetik,* 147.

10. Berg, "Die musikalische Impotenz der neuen Ästhetik Hans Pfitzners," 399–408.

11. Pfitzner, foreword to *Die neue Ästhetik,* 103–31.

12. Schering, "Geschichtliches zur 'ars inveniendi' in der Musik," 25–34.

13. Bahle, *Der musikalische Schaffensprozess.*

14. A note from 1945, quoted by Giselher Schubert in "'Vision' und 'Materialisation,'" 219.

15. See, for example, Schoenberg, "Composition with Twelve Tones."

16. Rufer, *Das Werk Arnold Schönbergs,* 26.

17. See for example, various texts in Rihm, *Ausgesprochen,* especially vol. 1; Jonathan Harvey offers several examples from Stockhausen's writings in his *Music and Inspiration,* see below.

18. Adorno, *Philosophie der neuen Musik,* 74, footnote 23.

19. Graf, *From Beethoven to Shostakovich,* 456.

20. See especially "Underground Games: The Importance of Dreaming," in Koestler, *The Act of Creation*, chap. 8.

21. I quote here from the back-cover summary, which offers a succinct version of the author's longer description on p. 55. See Duchesneau, *The Voice of the Muse*.

22. Harvey, *Music and Inspiration*, xvii.

23. Harvey, *Music and Inspiration*, xviii.

24. Harvey, *Music and Inspiration*, xix.

25. Dahlhaus, "Wagners Inspirationsmythen," 114.

26. Danuser and Katzenberger, *Vom Einfall zum Kunstwerk*.

27. Danuser, "Inspiration, Rationalität, Zufall," 11–21.

28. See, for example, the discussion of Berg's inspiration for his Violin Concerto in Stephan, "Von der Planung zum musikalischen Kunstwerk," 254.

Chapter One

1. Schumann, "Hector Berlioz," 49.

2. Schumann, "Hector Berlioz," 50.

3. Deathridge, "Life," 26.

4. Wagner, *Sämtliche Briefe*, 6:308–9.

5. Wagner, *Das braune Buch*, 122.

6. Wagner, *Mein Leben*, 511–12.

7. Wagner, *Mein Leben*, 561.

8. Dahlhaus, "Wagners Inspirationsmythen," 123–24.

9. See Deathridge, "Wagner's Sketches for the 'Ring,'" 387.

10. Schopenhauer, "Versuch über das Geistersehn," 262–63.

11. Schopenhauer, *Die Welt als Wille und Vorstellung*, 1:340.

12. Thayer, *Ludwig van Beethoven's Leben*, vol. 1.

13. Köchel, *Drei und achtzig neu aufgefundene Original-Briefe Ludwig van Beethovens an den Erzherzog Rudolph*; and Nohl, *Briefe Beethovens*.

14. Jahn, "Beethoven und die Ausgaben seiner Werke," 307–9.

15. Jahn, "Beethoven und die Ausgaben seiner Werke," 332–33.

16. Jahn, "Beethoven und die Ausgaben seiner Werke," 292.

17. Wagner, *Beethoven*, 28.

18. Wagner, *Beethoven*, 4.

19. Wagner, *Beethoven*, 28.

20. Wagner, *Beethoven*, 25.

21. Cosima Wagner, *Die Tagebücher* 1:917; entry for May 15, 1875.

22. Jahn, "Tannhäuser, Oper von Richard Wagner," 85–86.

23. Wagner, *Beethoven*, 35.

24. Wagner, *Beethoven*, 39.

25. Wagner, *Beethoven*, 13–14.

26. Wagner, *Beethoven*, 14.

27. Wagner, *Beethoven*, 15.

28. Wagner, *Beethoven*, 15.

29. Wagner, *Beethoven*, 40.

30. See especially "Underground Games: The Importance of Dreaming," in Koestler, *The Act of Creation*, chap. 8.

31. I am grateful to Roger Allen for bringing this to my attention.

32. Schopenhauer, "Versuch über das Geistersehn," 243.

33. Letter of April 9, 1858, quoted in Fehr, *Richard Wagners Schweizer Zeit*, 2:121.

34. Letter from Richter to Müller-Reuter of September 18, 1909, held by the Sächsische Landesbibliothek, Dresden, shelfmark Mscr. Dresd. A2551, 77.

35. Cosima Wagner, *Die Tagebücher*, 1:329–30; entry for December 25, 1870.

36. In 2009, the author had the opportunity of hearing the *Idyll* in Tribschen under the direction of Thomas Rösner, and was able to move from room to room to experience the impact of the villa's acoustic.

37. For a summary of the various references in Cosima's diaries and elsewhere to this passage and its conception, see Deathridge et al., *Wagner Werk-Verzeichnis (WWV)*, 508–9.

38. The issue has recently been subjected for the first time to convincing scholarly investigation. See Rieger, *"Leuchtende Liebe, lachender Tod,"* 210–27.

39. See the chapter "Voicing Mathilde: Wagner's Controlling Muse" in my *Richard Wagner's Zurich*, 201–42, esp. 212–14.

40. Cosima Wagner, *Die Tagebücher*, 1:1087; entry for November 19, 1877.

41. Cosima Wagner, *Die Tagebücher*, 2:133; entry for July 7, 1878.

42. Cosima Wagner, *Die Tagebücher*, 1:270; entry for August 15, 1870.

43. Cosima Wagner, *Die Tagebücher*, 1:323; entry for December 12, 1870.

44. See Walton: "Upstairs, Downstairs: Acoustics and Tempi in Wagner's 'Träume' and *Siegfried Idyll*."

45. Cosima Wagner, *Die Tagebücher*, 1:337; entry for January 4, 1871.

46. See Newman, *The Life of Richard Wagner*, vol. 4, *1866–1883*, 276.

47. Adorno, *Berg*, 348.

Chapter Two

1. See Mahler's letter to Friedrich Löhr of November 28, 1891, in Blaukopf, *Gustav Mahler Briefe*, 95.

2. Blaukopf, *Gustav Mahler Briefe*, 200.

3. The letter is quoted in Seidl, *Moderner Geist*, 60–61.

4. See, e.g., Mitchell, *Gustav Mahler*, and de La Grange, *Mahler*, vol. 1.

5. Ludwig Finscher, in an aside during a discussion of Dahlhaus's paper on "Wagner's inspiration myths" in Weimar in 1981, referred to the circumstances of

the inspiration for Mahler's last movement of the Second Symphony in a context that implicitly cast doubt on the story's veracity; but the discussion immediately moved on without any further mention of it. See the "Diskussion" in Goldschmidt, Knepler, and Niemann, *Komponisten auf Werk und Leben befragt*, 128.

6. Schoenberg, *Harmonielehre*, iii.

7. See, for example, Adorno's "Wiener Rede" or his "Epilegomena" with its musings on the expression of Mahler's death mask, both in *Quasi una Fantasia*.

8. A photograph of the plaque is available online at Gustav Mahler Vereinigung E. V., Hamburg, http://www.gustav-mahler-vereinigung.de/Bilder/Gedenktafel/body_gedenktafel.html (accessed July 2013).

9. Rosé, "Mahler und Hans von Bülow." We quote here from the printing in *Das Unterhaltungsblatt der Vossischen Zeitung*; the article also appeared in the *Neues Wiener Journal* and elsewhere. It is quoted at length in English in Mitchell, *Gustav Mahler*, 173.

10. Foerster, "Aus Mahlers Werkstatt," 923–24.

11. Foerster, "Z mých vzpomínek na Gustava Mahlera."

12. Stefan, *Gustav Mahler*, 34–35.

13. Foerster, "Erinnerungen an Gustav Mahler," 294.

14. Foerster, *Poutník v Hamburku*, 78. Also published in German translation in *Der Pilger: Erinnerungen eines Musikers*, 405.

15. Mahler, *"Liebste Justi!,"* 395.

16. See the facsimile in Karbusicky, *Mahler in Hamburg*, 154.

17. Mahler, *"Liebste Justi!,"* 395.

18. Reproduced on the jacket cover of Karbusicky, *Mahler in Hamburg*.

19. See Karbusicky, *Mahler in Hamburg*, esp. 128.

20. See Stockmann, "Ruht wohl, ihr teuren Gebeine," 463.

21. Mahler, *"Liebste Justi!,"* 383.

22. Rosé, "Mahler und Hans von Bülow."

23. Schabbing, *Gustav Mahler als Konzert- und Operndirigent*, 312.

24. Information kindly provided by Nele Tincheva, University of Hamburg, in an e-mail of June 14, 2011.

25. Schabbing, *Gustav Mahler als Konzert- und Operndirigent*, 18.

26. Mahler, *"Liebste Justi!,"* 384.

27. Seidl and Klatte, *Richard Strauss*, 1896.

28. Mahler's adverse comments on the letter's publication were recorded by Natalie Bauer-Lechner. See Killian, *Gustav Mahler in den Erinnerungen*, 170–71.

29. See, for example, *Römischer Katechismus Nach dem Beschlüsse des Konzils von Trient und auf Befehl des Papstes Pius V. herausgegeben*, 35.

30. See Schuhmann, "Arthur Seidl," 9.

31. See his various letters to Ödon von Mihalovich, Rosa Papier, Carl Goldmark, Wilhelm Jahn, and others as published in Mahler, *"Verehrter Herr College!,"* 169–96; the letter to Karpath is on 190–91.

32. See Nikkels, *"O Mensch! Gib Acht!,"* 66–67.

33. Floros, *Gustav Mahler*, 152–56.

34. Wagner, "Brief an einen italienischen Freund," 344.

35. See, for example, Bauer-Lechner, *Erinnerungen an Gustav Mahler*, 62–63.

36. Nikkels, *"O Mensch! Gib Acht!,"* 68–69.

37. Given in facsimile in Hefling, "Zweite Symphonie," 271.

38. See Hefling, "Content and context," 13–32, and Hefling, "Zweite Symphonie," 210–88.

39. Reik, *The Haunting Melody*, 269.

40. Zychowicz, "'They Only Give Rise to Misunderstandings,'" 153.

41. Blaukopf, *Gustav Mahler Briefe*, 28–29.

42. Blaukopf, *Gustav Mahler, Richard Strauss*, 24–28.

Chapter Three

Epigraph: Knaus, *Alban Berg*, 138.

1. See, for example, the facts as given in Floros, "Die Skizzen zum Violinkonzert," 118–19.

2. Reich, *Alban Berg*, 169.

3. Reich, "Requiem für Manon," 250–52; "Alban Bergs neues Werk" and "Alban Bergs neuestes Werk," 735–37. See also Reich, *Alban Berg* (1937), 126–33.

4. See Knaus and Sinkovicz, *Alban Berg*, 413.

5. Jarman, "Introduction," xiii.

6. See Berg, *Violinkonzert*, 9; and Jarman, "Secret Programmes," 171.

7. See Jarman, "Alban Berg, Wilhelm Fliess and the Secret Programme."

8. See Jarman, "Secret Programmes," 173–75.

9. See, for example, Brauneiss, "Form, Proportionen und Zahlen," esp. 243–44.

10. See Pople, *Berg: Violin Concerto*, 42; and Sartin, "Contagious Rhythm."

11. Krasner, "Origins of the Alban Berg Violin Concerto," 108. Helene Berg's claim is repeated variously in the literature and in popular sources, as for example in the German entry on Berg in *Wikipedia*, http://de.wikipedia.org/wiki/Alban_Berg (accessed October 2011).

12. See Brand, Hailey, and Meyer, *Briefwechsel Arnold Schönberg-Alban Berg*, 2:571.

13. Schoenberg, "Vortrag, zu halten in Frankfurt am Main," 26.

14. Schoenberg, "Vortrag, zu halten in Frankfurt am Main," 30.

15. Antony Beaumont has kindly pointed out that the passacaglia final movement of Zemlinsky's Symphony in B-flat Major might have been another model for Webern. Personal communication, July 2013.

16. This is all discussed in Knapp, "The Finale of Brahms's Fourth Symphony," 10.

17. See Reich, *Alban Berg* (1974), 100–101.

18. Fiedler, "Is This Enough?," 444–45, and Spitta, *Joh. Seb. Bach*, vol. 2, 294.

19. See Brand, Hailey, and Meyer, *Briefwechsel Arnold Schönberg-Alban Berg*, 2:430 and 504.

20. [Reich?], "Zur Entstehung des Violinkonzertes von Alban Berg," 196. See also Krasner, "The Origins of the Alban Berg Violin Concerto," 111.

21. See Brand, Hailey, and Meyer, *Briefwechsel Arnold Schönberg-Alban Berg*, 2:487.

22. Taruskin, *The Danger of Music*, 382.

23. See Hilmes, *Witwe im Wahn*, 180.

24. Letter from Krauss to Alma of March 3, 1933, in Steiger, *"Immer wieder werden,"* 478.

25. Hilmes, *Witwe im Wahn*, 277.

26. Thus Johannes Trentini, quoted by Hilmes in *Witwe im Wahn*, 271.

27. Canetti, "Begräbnis eines Engels," 202–7, esp. 204.

28. Karpath, "Manon Gropius."

29. Krenek, *Im Atem der Zeit*, 342. Krenek placed his memoirs in the Library of Congress to remain unread until fifteen years after his death. They have thus far been published only in German.

30. Krenek, *Im Atem der Zeit*, 342.

31. As recalled by Scholz in "More on Secret Programs" in Bruhn, *Encrypted Messages*, 52.

32. Undated letter after April 23, 1935; undated letter of late April 1935; undated letter of May 1935; undated letter of May or early June 1935; undated letter of mid-June 1935, in Steiger, *"Immer wieder werden,"* 232–36.

33. Quoted in Hilmes, *Witwe im Wahn*, 167.

34. Walter, *Thema und Variationen*, 411–12.

35. Canetti, "Begräbnis eines Engels" in *Das Augenspiel*, 202–7.

36. Walter Lindt, *Bruno Walter Briefe*, 241.

37. Steiger, *"Immer wieder werden,"* 188.

38. Knaus and Sinkovicz, *Alban Berg*, 410.

39. Adorno and Berg, *Briefwechsel 1925–1935*, 301.

40. Helene Berg, *Alban Berg: Briefe*, 615.

41. Helene Berg, *Alban Berg: Briefe*, 625.

42. Helene Berg, *Alban Berg: Briefe*, 626.

43. Helene Berg, *Alban Berg: Briefe*, 628.

44. Buchmayr, "Exil in Österreich?," 159.

45. Knaus and Sinkovicz, *Alban Berg*, 422–23.

46. Knaus and Leibnitz, *Altenberg bis Zuckerkandl*, 159. See also Knaus and Leibnitz, *Alban Berg*, 192–93.

47. Reich, "Ein Wiener Musiker übersetzt Mussolini," 107–9.

48. Mussolini, *Korporativer Staat*.

49. Letters held in the Rascher archives in the Zentralbibliothek Zürich.

50. Taruskin, *The Danger of Music*, 203.

51. See Notley, "1934, Alban Berg, and the Shadow of Politics," 226–27.

52. See the letter from Berg to Adorno of November 28, 1933, in Adorno and Berg, *Briefwechsel 1925–1935*, 286.

53. Notley, "1934, Alban Berg, and the Shadow of Politics," 236.

54. See Morgenstern, *Alban Berg und seine Idole*, 138.

55. Personal communication from Antony Beaumont, July 2013. Regarding Lulu/Alma and the Painter/Kokoschka, see Botstein, "Alban Berg and the Memory of Modernism," 310.

56. Steiger, *"Immer wieder werden,"* 454.

57. Jarman, "Secret Programmes," 175.

58. [Reich?], "Alban Bergs Requiem für Manon," 233.

59. Letter from Berg to Adorno of November 2, 1935, in Adorno and Berg, *Briefwechsel 1925–1935*, 324.

60. See Dalen, "Freundschaft, Liebe, und Welt."

61. Derrick Puffett, "Berg's Reception of Schoenberg's *Pelleas und Melisande*," 585–86.

62. See Jarman, "Alban Berg, Wilhelm Fliess and the Secret Programme."

63. Brand, Hailey, and Meyer, *Briefwechsel Arnold Schönberg-Alban Berg*, 2:267.

64. See Adorno and Berg, *Briefwechsel 1925–1935*, 333. On Adorno's hankering to hobnob with the titled classes, see Hagedorn, "Der Unbeugsame."

65. Steiger, *"Immer wieder werden,"* 511.

66. Floros, *Alban Berg und Hanna Fuchs*, 34.

67. Letter written from Berg to Hanna Fuchs after July 11 and before July 23, 1925, in Floros, *Alban Berg und Hanna Fuchs*, 29–40, here 35.

68. Floros, *Alban Berg und Hanna Fuchs*, 36.

69. See Floros, *Alban Berg und Hanna Fuchs*, 65–69; and Golther, *Richard Wagner an Mathilde Wesendonk*, 26–30, esp. 27.

70. See Floros, *Alban Berg und Hanna Fuchs*, 50–55, esp. 53.

71. Perle, "The Secret Programme."

72. See, for example, the various contributions in Bruhn, *Encrypted Messages in Alban Berg's Music*.

73. For more detail, see the article and bibliography of Tatlow and Griffiths, "Numbers and Music."

74. One might even argue that this musicological fascination was itself a symptom of the broader obsession with "secret knowledge" evident in the popular media in the 1970s, as proven by the million-dollar success of Erich von Däniken's cosmic palaeontology or the flurry surrounding the story of "Enigma" and the World War II code-breakers of Bletchley Park. But to suggest such connections might be to indulge in the selfsame urge to discover hidden links between things that are in fact unconnected.

75. The drawing is given in facsimile in Knaus and Leibnitz, *Alban Berg*, 258.

76. See Steiger, *"Immer wieder werden,"* 213–16.

77. Knaus and Leibnitz, *Alban Berg: Briefentwürfe*, 138. See also Steiger, *"Immer wieder werden,"* 107.

78. Knaus and Leibnitz, *Alban Berg: Briefentwürfe*, 94.

79. Kindly confirmed by Thomas Leibnitz of the Austrian National Library.

80. Floros, *Alban Berg und Hanna Fuchs*, 87–88.

81. Knaus and Leibnitz, *Altenberg bis Zuckerkandl*, 225–27.

82. Letter of late March 1933 to Anny Askenase in Knaus and Leibnitz, *Altenberg bis Zuckerkandl*, 221–22.

83. See Berg's letter to Hanna of December 14, 1934, and to Edith Edwards of February 1935, in Floros, *Alban Berg und Hanna Fuchs*, 89–90 and Knaus and Leibnitz, *Altenberg bis Zuckerkandl*, 228.

84. See Haefeli, *IGNM: Die Internationale Gesellschaft für Neue Musik*, 248.

85. Adorno, *Berg: Der Meister des kleinen Übergangs*, 367.

86. Adorno, *Berg: Der Meister des kleinen Übergangs*, 364.

87. See the descriptions in Pople, *Berg: Violin Concerto*, 42.

88. Knaus and Leibnitz, *Altenberg bis Zuckerkandl*, 427 and 439n65.

89. Letter from Berg to Alma Mahler of December 30, 1919, in Steiger, *"Immer wieder werden,"* 82.

90. Brand, Hailey, and Meyer, *Briefwechsel Arnold Schönberg-Alban Berg*, 2:120.

91. Brand, Hailey, and Meyer, *Briefwechsel Arnold Schönberg-Alban Berg*, 2:570–72.

92. Brand, Hailey, and Meyer, *Briefwechsel Arnold Schönberg-Alban Berg*, 2:575.

93. Letter from Berg to Adorno of July 4, 1935, in Adorno and Berg, *Briefwechsel 1925–1935*, 320.

94. Letter from Berg to Ingeborg and Soma Morgenstern of June 4, 1935, in Morgenstern, *Alban Berg und seine Idole*, 278.

95. Reich, *Alban Berg* (1963), 169. See also Reich, *Alban Berg* (1937), 127.

96. Reich, "Requiem für Manon," 251.

97. Adorno and Berg, *Briefwechsel*, 300.

98. See, for example, the children's pictures drawn after a performance of the Violin Concerto by the Heidelberg Philharmonic in 2005 online at http://www.heidelberger-philharmoniker.de/index.php?id=423 (accessed February 2011).

99. Graubart, review of David Gable and Robert Morgan, *Alban Berg*, 40.

100. Perle, "The Secret Programme," 812.

101. Perle, *Lulu*, 26.

102. See Floros, *Alban Berg und Hanna Fuchs*, 87.

103. See Brand, Hailey, and Meyer, *Briefwechsel Arnold Schönberg-Alban Berg*, 1:267–71, esp. 269; and Pople, "In the Orbit of *Lulu*," esp. ex. 11.6d on 214.

104. Reich, *Alban Berg* (1937), 133.

105. See Lang, "Fragment zu Kokoschka," 50.

106. Berg, Alma, and Kokoschka were among the signatories of a congratulatory, postconcert card sent to Schoenberg on June 29, 1912. See Brand, Hailey, and Meyer, *Briefwechsel Arnold Schönberg-Alban Berg*, 1:246–47.

107. Letter from Kokoschka to Will Grohmann, December 7, 1951, in Kokoschka and Spielmann, *Oskar Kokoschka*, 258.

108. See Bekker, "Zu Kokoschkas Bach-Kantate," 32.

Chapter Four

1. For a discussion of assorted reasons for writer's blocks, including "oral-masochistic conflicts," see Rose, *Writer's Block*, here esp. 13.

2. Furtwängler, *Briefe*, 78.

3. Elisabeth Furtwängler, *Über Wilhelm Furtwängler*, 16.

4. See Trémine, *Wilhelm Furtwängler*, 45.

5. See, for example, Stresemann, . . . *und abends in die Philharmonie*, 51.

6. See, for example, Listewnik and Sander, *Wilhelm Furtwängler*, 57.

7. Wilhem Furtwängler, *Lieder, Te Deum, Religioser Hymnus*, Frankfurt Philharmonic Orchestra, Oder, Frankfurt Singakademie, dir. Alfred Walter, sung by Guido Pikal, Marco Polo 8.223546.

8. Wilhem Furtwängler, *Symphony in D Major, Symphony in B Minor*, Slovak State Philharmonic, Kosice, dir. Alfred Walter, Marco Polo 8.223645.

9. Behr, *Denkschrift*, 65.

10. See Haffner, *Furtwängler*, 34–35.

11. Wilhem Furtwängler, *Symphony in D Major, Symphony in B Minor*, Slovak State Philharmonic, Kosice, dir. Alfred Walter, Marco Polo 8.223645.

12. Schmitz, review of "Adagio" for orchestra, 332.

13. Elisabeth Furtwängler, *Über Wilhelm Furtwängler*, 17.

14. Furtwängler, *Briefe*, 63.

15. Furtwängler, *Briefe*, 69.

16. Furtwängler, *Briefe*, 74–75.

17. For a mention of the "Führer unserer Philharmoniker" see, for example, the "Unterhaltungsblatt" of the *Vossische Zeitung* of April 19, 1932 (almost a year before another "Führer" took political office in the German state).

18. See, for example, Haffner, *Furtwängler*, 123–30 and 196.

19. For example, in "Wenn die Kritik der Presse für das Musikleben ausscheidet." A typescript is in Furtwängler's archives with a handwritten remark on it: "Handed to Minister Goebbels 1937."

20. See Brotbeck, "Alles sehr allmählich," esp. 44–51.

21. See Brotbeck, "Alles sehr allmählich," 49.

22. See the list of Furtwängler's writings in the catalogue of his archives: Nachl. W. Furtwängler, "Nachlassverzeichnis: Wilhelm Furtwängler (1886–1954)," where there are, for example, various versions and variations of the essay published variously as "Der Musiker und sein Publikum" and "Chaos und Gestalt" (see below).

23. Furtwängler, *Der Musiker und sein Publikum*, 21.

24. Furtwängler, *Der Musiker und sein Publikum*, 17.

25. Furtwängler, *Der Musiker und sein Publikum*, 16.
26. Furtwängler, *Der Musiker und sein Publikum*, 17.
27. Furtwängler, *Der Musiker und sein Publikum*, 33.
28. Furtwängler, *Der Musiker und sein Publikum*, 18.
29. See Pfitzner, *Über musikalische Inspiration*.
30. Furtwängler, *Der Musiker und sein Publikum*, 36.
31. Drüner, *Schöpfer und Zerstörer*, 265–80.
32. See Trémine, *Wilhelm Furtwängler*, 57–68.

Chapter Five

1. See, for example, Robin Holloway's article on *Capriccio* in his *On Music*, 142–49.
2. Garlington, "Richard Strauss's 'Vier letzte Lieder,'" 79.
3. Schuh, "Strauss during the War Years," 9.
4. Gilliam and Youmans, "Strauss, Richard."
5. Kennedy, "Strauss's Autumn Glory," 19.
6. The various articles listed in these notes offer numerous examples.
7. Strauss, "Erinnerungen an meinen Vater," 194.
8. Strauss, "Künstlerisches Vermächtnis."
9. The documentation for this "Führerentscheid" is only extant in the case of Richard Junior, though was presumably also arranged for Christian. The "Arisierung" took place on April 22, 1941. I am grateful to Gerhard Splitt for sharing this information with me.
10. Personal communication, Zurich, April 1986.
11. Walter Adolf Jöhr, *America und der Faschismus*.
12. Zurlinden, "Einige Briefe von Richard Strauss," 12–14.
13. Adolf Jöhr, "Reminiscences of Richard Strauss."
14. Kennedy, *Richard Strauss: Man, Musician, Enigma*, 372–73.
15. Schuh, "Strauss during the War Years," 8–10.
16. Schuh, "Strauss during the War Years," 10.
17. See Roth, "Richard Strauss in London 1947," 132–40.
18. "Richard Strauss Festival," *Times*, October 21, 1947.
19. Adolf Jöhr, "Reminiscences of Richard Strauss."
20. Strauss, Stravinsky, and Kodály, "Correspondence with Dr. Roth," 11.
21. See my chapter on Strauss's late operas in a forthcoming handbook on Richard Strauss, edited by Tim Jackson.
22. Friedelind Wagner and Cooper, *Heritage of Fire*, 92. See also Rieger, *Friedelind Wagner*, 173.
23. William McNaught, "The Promenades," 316.
24. Information kindly provided by Ray Holden.

25. Tenschert, "Richard Strauss' Schwanengesang," 182–86; Frank, "Strauss's Last Songs," 305; Hutchings, "Strauss's 'Four Last Songs,'" 465; Kennedy, "Strauss's Autumn Glory," 19; Schuh, "Richard Strauss's 'Four Last Songs,'" 29; and Garlington, "Richard Strauss's 'Vier letzte Lieder,'" 92.

26. Schuh, "Richard Strauss's 'Four Last Songs,'" 29–30.

27. See, for example, the articles of Hutchings, Kennedy, and Schuh mentioned above.

28. Schuh, "Richard Strauss's 'Four Last Songs,'" 26.

29. Roth, "Richard Strauss in London 1947," 137.

30. Letter from Strauss to Willi Schuh of December 12, 1943, in Strauss, *Briefwechsel mit Willi Schuh*, 57.

31. Jackson, "*Ruhe, meine Seele!*," 90–137.

32. See Schaal, "Abschied vom Leben," 549.

33. Frank, "Strauss's Last Songs," 305.

34. Heaney, "The Baler," in *Human Chain*, 24–25.

35. Sutcliffe, "Are We Still Backing the Wrong Horse?"

36. I am grateful to Ray Holden for pointing this out to me.

37. For instance, Claudio Abbado and Karita Mattila with the Berlin Philharmonic on Deutsche Grammophon.

38. Strauss, "Vom melodischen Einfall," 163–64. Emphasis in original.

39. Wagner, *Beethoven*, esp. 8–18.

Postlude

1. Burgess, "The Art of Fiction No. 48."

2. Stravinsky and Craft, *Conversations with Igor Stravinsky*, 17–18.

3. Stravinsky and Craft, *Expositions and Developments*, 147–48.

4. Nyffeler, "Rolf Liebermann (1910–1999)." Anne Shreffler has noted that Stravinsky was first offered $5,000 plus a conducting fee of $2,500. She also offers convincing proof that the funds for the commission were channeled only through Hamburg but actually came from the CIA-funded "Congress for Cultural Freedom" of which Nabokov was the Secretary General. This could also explain why the extra money Stravinsky demanded was so easily procured. However, Shreffler also observes that it is unclear whether Nabokov was aware of the funding role of the CIA. See Shreffler, "Ideologies of Serialism," 229 and 244n44.

5. This is quoted so often that it is probably not apocryphal, though the present writer has not found a definitive source. Others have offered similar answers to the same question; Stephen Sondheim recalls Richard Rodgers' reply as being "the check." See Lipton, "Stephen Sondheim, The Art of the Musical."

6. Schering, "Geschichtliches zur 'ars inveniendi' in der Musik."

7. There is also a more banal flipside to an insistence on music's transcendent inspiration. No one finds it odd that architects or carpenters should be paid a fair wage. But the growth of the "inspiration myth" is surely in large part responsible for the often inadequate commission sums paid to composers, even for works that might have taken months to draft and score. The market has in large part interiorized the notion of composers being "inspired" and generally finds it odd to pay generously for something that the composer himself has implicitly received "for free" through some quasi-divine gift, or that his inner "daemon" would have compelled him to write in any case.

8. Cosima Wagner, *Die Tagebücher*, 2:335, entry for April 22, 1879.

9. Pfitzner, *Über musikalische Inspiration*, esp. 13–15 and 88–89.

10. Ballantine, "Joseph Shabalala," 5–6.

11. See, e.g., Walter and Fridman, *Shamanism*, 1:180; and Spalding, "You and I and Nobody Knows," 9–10.

BIBLIOGRAPHY

Adorno, Theodor Wiesengrund. *Berg: Der Meister des kleinen Übergangs*. In *Die Musikalischen Monographien*. Frankfurt am Main: Suhrkamp, 1986.

———. *Philosophie der neuen Musik*. Frankfurt am Main: Suhrkamp, 1978.

———. *Quasi una Fantasia*. Frankfurt: Suhrkamp, 1963.

Adorno, Theodor Wiesengrund, and Alban Berg. *Briefwechsel 1925–1935*. Edited by Henri Lonitz. Frankfurt am Main: Suhrkamp, 1997.

Anonymous. *Römischer Kathechismus Nach dem Beschlusse des Konzils von Trient und auf Befehl des Papstes Pius V. herausgegeben*. Passau: Friedrich Winkler, 1839.

Bahle, Julius. *Der musikalische Schaffensprozess: Psychologie der schöpferischen Erlebnis- und Antriebsformen*. Constance: Paul Christiani, 1947.

Ballantine, Christopher. "Joseph Shabalala: Chronicles of an African Composer." *British Journal of Ethnomusicology* 5 (1996): 1–38.

Bauer-Lechner, Natalie. *Erinnerungen an Gustav Mahler*. Leipzig, Germany: Tal & Co., 1923.

Behr, Hermann. *Denkschrift zur Feier des 50jährigen Bestehens des Breslauer Orchester-Vereins E.V.* Breslau: Korn, 1912.

Bekker, Paul. "Die musikalische Impotenz der neuen Ästhetik Hans Pfitzners." *Musikblätter des Anbruch* 11/12 (1920): 399–408.

———. "Zu Kokoschkas Bach-Kantate." In Kokoschka, *O Ewigkeit, du Donnerwort*, 31–36.

Berg, Alban. *Konzerte*. Vol. 5 of *Musikalische Werke*. Section 1 of *Sämtliche Werke*. Edited by Douglas Jarman. Vienna: Universal Edition, 1996.

———. *Violinkonzert: "Dem Angedenken eines Engels"; Faksimile nach dem Autograph der Library of Congress, Washington*. Edited by Douglas Jarman. Laaber, Germany: Laaber-Verlag, 2011.

Berg, Helene. *Alban Berg: Briefe an seine Frau*. Munich, Vienna: Langen, Müller, 1965.

Berger, Karol, and Anthony Newcomb, eds. *Music and the Aesthetics of Modernity: Essays*. Cambridge, MA: Harvard University Department of Music, 2005.

Blaukopf, Herta, ed. *Gustav Mahler Briefe*. Vienna: Zsolnay, 1982.

———, ed. *Gustav Mahler, Richard Strauss: Briefwechsel 1888–1911.* Munich: Piper, 1988.

Botstein, Leon. "Alban Berg and the Memory of Modernism." In Hailey, *Alban Berg and His World*, 299–334.

Brand, Juliane, Christopher Hailey, and Andreas Meyer. *Briefwechsel Arnold Schönberg-Alban Berg.* 2 vols. Mainz, Germany: Schott, 2007.

Brauneiss, Leo. "Form, Proportionen und Zahlen in Alban Bergs 'Violinkonzert.'" In *Jahrbuch des Staatlichen Instituts für Musikforschung Preussischer Kulturbesitz 2003*, edited by Günther Wagner, 224–48. Stuttgart: Metzler, 2003.

Brotbeck, Roman. "Alles sehr allmählich: Anmerkungen zum Komponisten Wilhelm Furtwängler." In *Wilhelm Furtwängler in Diskussion*, edited by Chris Walton, 41–55. Winterthur, Switzerland: Amadeus Verlag, 1996.

Bruhn, Siglind, ed. *Encrypted Messages in Alban Berg's Music.* New York: Garland, 1998.

Buchmayr, Friedrich. "Exil in Österreich? Johannes Hollnsteiners Engagement für Thomas Mann: Mit zwei unveröffentlichten Briefen Thomas Manns." In vol. 13 of *Thomas Mann Jahrbuch*, 147–73. Frankfurt am Main: Klostermann, 2001.

Burgess, Anthony. "The Art of Fiction No. 48." Interview with John Cullinan. *Paris Review*, no. 56 (1973). http://www.theparisreview.org/interviews/3994/the-art-of-fiction-no-48-anthony-burgess.

Canetti, Elias. "Begräbnis eines Engels." In *Das Augenspiel.* Berlin: Verlag Volk und Welt, 1986.

Dahlhaus, Carl. "Wagners Inspirationsmythen." In *Komponisten auf Werk und Leben befragt: Ein Kolloquium*, edited by Harry Goldschmidt, Georg Knepler, and Konrad Niemann, 108–25. Leipzig, Germany: VEB Deutscher Verlag für Musik, 1985.

Dalen, Brenda. "Freundschaft, Liebe, und Welt: The Secret Programme of the Chamber Concerto." In *The Berg Companion*, edited by Douglas Jarman, 141–80. Basingstoke: Macmillan, 1989.

Danuser, Hermann. "Inspiration, Rationalität, Zufall: Über musikalische Poetik im 20. Jahrhundert." In *Vom Einfall zum Kunstwerk*, edited by Hermann Danuser and Günter Katzenberger, 11–21. Laaber, Germany: Laaber-Verlag, 1993.

Danuser, Hermann, and Günter Katzenberger, eds. *Vom Einfall zum Kunstwerk: Der Kompositionsprozess in der Musik des 20. Jahrhunderts.* Laaber, Germany: Laaber-Verlag, 1993.

Deathridge, John. "Life." In *The New Grove Wagner*, edited by John Deathridge and Carl Dahlhaus, 1–66. London: Macmillan, 1984.

———. "Wagner's Sketches for the 'Ring': Some Recent Studies." *Musical Times* 118, no. 1611 (1977): 387.

Deathridge, John, Martin Geck, Egon Voss, and Isolde Vetter. *Wagner Werk-Verzeichnis (WWV).* Mainz, Germany: Schott, 1986.

de La Grange, Henry-Louis. *Mahler.* Vol. 1. Garden City, NY: Doubleday, 1973.

Drüner, Ulrich. *Schöpfer und Zerstörer: Richard Wagner als Künstler*. Cologne: Böhlau Verlag, 2003.

Duchesneau, Louise. *The Voice of the Muse: A Study of the Role of Inspiration in Musical Composition*. Frankfurt am Main: Peter Lang, 1986.

Fehr, Max. *Richard Wagners Schweizer Zeit*. 2 vols. Aarau, Switzerland: Sauerländer, 1934–53.

Fiedler, Achim. "Is This Enough?" *Musical Times* 134, no. 1806 (1993): 444–45.

Fischer, Jens Malte. *Gustav Mahler: Der fremde Vertraute*. Vienna: Paul Zsolnay Verlag, 2003.

Floros, Constantin. *Alban Berg und Hanna Fuchs: Die Geschichte einer Liebe in Briefen*. Zurich: Arche, 2001.

———. *Gustav Mahler: I: Die geistige Welt Gustav Mahlers in systematischer Darstellung*. Wiesbaden: Breitkopf & Härtel, 1977.

———. "Die Skizzen zum Violinkonzert von Alban Berg." In *Alban Berg Symposion Wien 1980: Tagungsbericht*. Vol. 2 of *Alban Berg Studien*, edited by Rudolf Klein, 118–35. Vienna: Universal Edition, 1981.

Foerster, Josef. "Aus Mahlers Werkstatt: Erinnerungen." *Der Merker* 1, no. 23 (1910): 923–24.

———. "Erinnerungen an Gustav Mahler." *Musikblätter des Anbruch* 2, nos. 7/8 (1920): 291–95.

———. *Der Pilger: Erinnerungen eines Musikers*. Prague: Artia, 1955.

———. *Poutník v Hamburku*. Prague: Sfinx, 1939.

———. "Z mých vzpomínek na Gustava Mahlera." *Smetana* 1 (1911): 264–66.

Frank, Alan. "Strauss's Last Songs." *Music & Letters* 31, no. 4 (1950): 305–6.

Furtwängler, Elisabeth. *Über Wilhelm Furtwängler*. Wiesbaden: Brockhaus, 1979.

Furtwängler, Nachl. W. "Nachlassverzeichnis: Wilhelm Furtwängler (1886–1954)." Zurich: Zentralbibliothek Zürich, 2009. http://www.zb.uzh.ch/Medien/spezialsammlungen/musik/nachlaesse/furtwaenglerwilhelm.pdf.

Furtwängler, Wilhelm. *Briefe*. Edited by Frank Theiss. 3rd ed. Wiesbaden: Brockhaus, 1965.

———. *Der Musiker und sein Publikum*. Zurich: Atlantis, 1955.

Garlington, Aubrey S., Jr. "Richard Strauss's 'Vier letzte Lieder': The Ultimate 'Opus Ultimum.'" *Musical Quarterly* 73, no. 1 (1989): 79–93.

Gilliam, Bryan, ed. *Richard Strauss and His World*. Princeton, NJ: Princeton University Press, 1992.

Gilliam, Bryan, and Charles Youmans. "Strauss, Richard." In *Grove Music Online*. Oxford University Press. Accessed July 2013.

Goldschmidt, Harry, Georg Knepler, and Konrad Niemann, eds. *Komponisten auf Werk und Leben befragt: Ein Kolloquium*. Leipzig, Germany: VEB Deutscher Verlag für Musik, 1985.

Golther, Wolfgang, ed. *Richard Wagner an Mathilde Wesendonk: Tagebuchblätter und Briefe 1853–1871*. Leipzig, Germany: Breitkopf & Härtel, 1912.

Graf, Max. *From Beethoven to Shostakovich: The Psychology of the Composing Process*. New York: Greenwood Press, 1947.

Graubart, Michael. Review of *Alban Berg: Historical and Analytical Perspectives*, by David Gable and Robert Morgan, and *Berg: Violin Concerto*, by Anthony Pople. *Tempo*, no. 180 (1992): 36–41.

Haefeli, Anton. *IGNM: Die Internationale Gesellschaft für Neue Musik; Ihre Geschichte von 1922 bis zur Gegenwart*. Zurich: Atlantis Musikbuch-Verlag, 1982.

Haffner, Herbert. *Furtwängler*. Berlin: Parthas Verlag/Arte Edition, 2003.

Hagedorn, Volker. "Der Unbeugsame." Interview with Michael Gielen. *Die Zeit*, April 29, 2010. http://www.zeit.de/2010/18/Gespraech-Michael-Gielen.

Hailey, Christopher, ed. *Alban Berg and His World*. Princeton, NJ: Princeton University Press, 2010.

Harvey, Jonathan. *Music and Inspiration*. London: Faber & Faber, 1999.

Hausegger, Friedrich von, "Aus dem Jenseits des Künstlers." In *Gedanken eines Schauenden: Gesammelte Aufsätze*, edited by Siegmund von Hausegger, 362–424. Munich: Bruckmann, 1903.

Heaney, Seamus. *Human Chain*. London: Faber & Faber, 2010.

Hefling, Stephen E. "Content and Context of the Sketches." In *Mahler: The Resurrection Chorale*, edited by Gilbert E. Kaplan, 13–32. New York: Kaplan Foundation, 1994.

———. "Zweite Symphonie." In vol. 1 of *Gustav Mahler: Interpretationen seiner Werke*, edited by Peter Revers and Oliver Korte, 210–88. Laaber, Germany: Laaber-Verlag, 2011.

Hilmes, Oliver. *Witwe im Wahn: Das Leben der Alma Mahler-Werfel*. Munich: Pantheon Verlag, 2010.

Hindemith, Paul. *Komponist in seiner Welt: Weiten und Grenzen*. Zurich: Atlantis, 1959.

Holloway, Robin. *On Music: Essays and Diversions 1963–2003*. Brinkworth, UK: Claridge Press, 2003.

Hutchings, Arthur. "Strauss's 'Four Last Songs.'" *Musical Times* 91, no. 1294 (1950): 465–68.

Jackson, Timothy L. "*Ruhe, meine Seele!* and the *Letzte Orchesterlieder*." In *Richard Strauss and His World*, edited by Bryan Gilliam, 90–137. Princeton, NJ: Princeton University Press, 1992.

Jahn, Otto. "Beethoven und die Ausgaben seiner Werke." In *Gesammelte Aufsätze über Musik*, edited by Otto Jahn, 271–337. Leipzig, Germany: Breitkopf & Härtel, 1866.

———. "Tannhäuser, Oper von Richard Wagner." In *Gesammelte Aufsätze über Musik*, edited by Otto Jahn, 64–86. Leipzig, Germany: Breitkopf & Härtel, 1866.

Jarman, Douglas. "Alban Berg, Wilhelm Fliess and the Secret Programme of the Violin Concerto." *Musical Times* 124, no. 1682 (1983): 218–23.

————. Introduction to *Konzerte*. Vol. 5 of *Musikalische Werke*. Section 1 of *Sämtliche Werke* by Alban Berg, edited by Douglas Jarman, xiii–[xvii]. Vienna: Universal Edition, 1996.

————. *The Music of Alban Berg*. London: Faber & Faber, 1983.

————. "Secret Programmes." In Pople, *The Cambridge Companion to Berg*, 167–79.

Jarman, Douglas, ed. *The Berg Companion*. Basingstoke: Macmillan, 1989.

Jöhr, Adolf. "Reminiscences of Richard Strauss." Manuscript held by the Richard Strauss Institut, Garmisch-Partenkirchen.

Jöhr, Walter Adolf. *America und der Faschismus*. Berne, Switzerland: Paul Haupt, 1937.

Kaplan, Gilbert E., ed. *Mahler: The Resurrection Chorale*. New York: Kaplan Foundation, 1994.

Karbusicky, Vladimir. *Mahler in Hamburg: Chronik einer Freundschaft*. Hamburg: von Bockel, 1996.

Karpath, Ludwig. "Manon Gropius: Ein Wort des Gedenkens" in *Wiener Sonn-und Montags-Zeitung* 73, no. 17 (1935): 9.

Kennedy, Michael. *Richard Strauss: Man, Musician, Enigma*. Cambridge: Cambridge University Press, 2006.

————. "Strauss's Autumn Glory." *Tempo*, 2nd ser., no. 210 (1999): 17–19.

Killian, Herbert, ed. *Gustav Mahler in den Erinnerungen von Natalie Bauer-Lechner*. Hamburg: Wagner, 1984.

Kinderman, William, and Joseph E. Jones, eds. *Genetic Criticsm and the Creative Process: Essays from Music, Literature, and Theater*. Rochester, NY: University of Rochester Press, 2009.

Klein, Rudolf, ed. *Alban Berg Symposion Wien 1980: Tagungsbericht*. Vol. 2 of *Alban Berg Studien*. Vienna: Universal Edition, 1981.

Knapp, Raymond. "The Finale of Brahms's Fourth Symphony: The Tale of the Subject." *19th-Century Music* 13, no. 1 (1989): 3–17.

Knaus, Herwig, ed. *Alban Berg: Handschriftliche Briefe, Briefentwürfe und Notizen; Aus den Beständen der Musiksammlung der Österreichischen Nationalbibliothek*. Wilhelmshaven: Florian Noetzel Verlag, 2004.

Knaus, Herwig, and Thomas Leibnitz, eds. *Alban Berg: Briefentwürfe, Aufzeichnungen, Familienbriefe, das "Bergwerk"; Aus den Beständen der Musiksammlung der Österreichischen Nationalbibliothek*. Wilhelmshaven: Florian Noetzel Verlag, 2004.

————. *Alban Berg: Maschinenschriftliche und handschriftliche Briefe, Briefentwürfe, Skizzen und Notizen; Aus den Beständem der Musiksammlung der Österreichischen Nationalbibliothek*. Wilhelmshaven: Florian Noetzel Verlag, 2005.

————. *Altenberg bis Zuckerkandl: Briefe an Alban Berg; Liebesbriefe von Alban Berg; Aus den Beständen der Österreichischen Nationalbibliothek*. Vienna: Erhard Löcker, 2009.

Knaus, Herwig, and Wilhelm Sinkovicz. *Alban Berg: Zeitumstände—Lebenslinien.* St. Pölten: Residenz Verlag, 2008.

Köchel, Ludwig von, ed. *Drei und achtzig neu aufgefundene Original-Briefe Ludwig van Beethovens an den Erzherzog Rudolph.* Vienna: Beck'sche Universitätsbuchhandlung, 1865.

Koestler, Arthur. *The Act of Creation.* London: Hutchinson, 1964.

Kokoschka, Olda, and Heinz Spielmann, eds. *Oskar Kokoschka: Briefe III; 1934–1953.* Düsseldorf: Claassen, 1986.

Kokoschka, Oskar, ed. *O Ewigkeit, du Donnerwort: 11 Lithographien und die Vorzeichnungen zur Kantata von Johann Sebastian Bach.* Leipzig, Germany: Philipp Reclam jun., 1984.

Krasner, Louis. "The Origins of the Alban Berg Violin Concerto." In *Alban Berg Symposion Wien 1980: Tagungsbericht,* edited by Rudolf Klein, 107–17. Vienna: Universal Edition, 1981.

Krenek, Ernst. *Im Atem der Zeit: Erinnerungen an die Moderne.* Translated by Friedrich Saathen and Sabine Schulte. Hamburg: Hoffmann und Campe, 1998.

Lang, Lothar. "Fragment zu Kokoschka." In Kokoschka, *O Ewigkeit, du Donnerwort,* 44–54.

Langer, Axel, and Chris Walton. *Minne, Muse und Mäzen: Otto und Mathilde Wesendonck und ihr Zürcher Künstlerzirkel.* Zurich: Museum Rietberg, 2002.

Lipton, James. "Stephen Sondheim, The Art of the Musical." Paris Review, no. 142 (Spring 1997). http://www.theparisreview.org/interviews/1283/ the-art-of-the-musical-stephen-sondheim.

Listewnik, Arnd-Volker, and Hedwig Sander. *Wilhelm Furtwängler.* Leipzig, Germany: Edition Peters, 1986.

Mahler, Gustav. *Gustav Mahler Briefe.* Edited by Herta Blaukopf. Vienna: Zsolnay, 1982.

———. *"Liebste Justi!": Briefe an die Familie.* Edited by Herta Blaukopf. Bonn: Weidle Verlag, 2006.

———. *"Verehrter Herr College!": Briefe an Komponisten, Dirigenten, Intendanten.* Edited by Herta Blaukopf. Vienna: Paul Zsolnay Verlag, 2010.

McNaught, William. "The Promenades." *Musical Times* 87, no. 1244 (1946): 316.

Mitchell, Donald. *Gustav Mahler: The Wunderhorn Years.* Berkeley: University of California Press, 1995.

Morgenstern, Soma. *Alban Berg und seine Idole: Erinnerungen und Briefe.* Edited by Ingolf Schulte. Lüneburg: zu Klampen, 1995.

Mussolini, Benito. *Korporativer Staat: Mit einem Anhang; Die geistigen Grundlagen des Korporations-Systems von Wilhelm Reich.* Translated by Wilhelm [Willi] Reich. Zurich: Rascher & Cie, 1934.

Newman, Ernest. *The Life of Richard Wagner.* Vol. 4, *1866–1883.* Cambridge: Cambridge University Press, 1976.

Nikkels, Eveline. *"O Mensch! Gib Acht!": Friedrich Nietzsches Bedeutung für Gustav Mahler*. Amsterdam: Rodopi, 1989.

Nohl, Ludwig, ed. *Briefe Beethovens*. Stuttgart: Cotta, 1865.

Notley, Margaret. "1934, Alban Berg, and the Shadow of Politics: Documents of a Troubled Year." In Hailey, *Alban Berg and his World*, 223–68.

Nottebohm, Gustav. *Ein Skizzenbuch von Beethoven: Beschrieben und in Auszügen dargestellt*. Leipzig, Germany: Breitkopf & Härtel, 1865.

Nyffeler, Max. "Rolf Liebermann (1910–1999), ein Zeitzeuge des 20. Jahrhunderts: Stationen aus seinem bewegten Leben." Accessed July 2013. http://www.beck-messer.de/komponisten/liebermann/portrait.html.

Perle, George. *Lulu*. Vol. 2 of *The Operas of Alban Berg*. Berkeley: University of California Press, 1985.

———. "The Secret Programme of the Lyric Suite." Pts. 1–3. *Musical Times* 118, no. 1614 (1977): 629–32; no. 1615 (1977): 709–13; no. 1616 (1977): 809–13.

Pfitzner, Hans. Foreword to *Die neue Ästhetik der musikalischen Impotenz: Ein Verwesungssymptom?* 3rd ed. In vol. 2 of *Gesammelte Schriften*, 103–31. Augsburg: Benno Filser-Verlag, 1926.

———. *Die neue Aesthetik der musikalischen Impotenz: Ein Verwesungssymptom?* Munich: Verlag der Süddeutschen Monatshefte, 1920.

———. *Über musikalische Inspiration*. 4th ed. Berlin-Grunewald: Johannes Oertel, 1943.

Pople, Anthony. *Berg: Violin Concerto*. Cambridge: Cambridge University Press, 1991.

———. "In the Orbit of *Lulu*: The Late Works." In Pople, *The Cambridge Companion to Berg*, 204–26.

Pople, Anthony, ed. *The Cambridge Companion to Berg*. Cambridge: Cambridge University Press, 1997.

Puffett, Derrick. "Berg's Reception of Schoenberg's *Pelleas und Melisande*." In *Derrick Puffett on Music*, edited by Kathryn Bailey Puffett, 539–615. Aldershot, UK: Ashgate, 2001.

Reich, Willi. *Alban Berg*. Vienna: Herbert Reichner, 1937.

———. *Alban Berg*. New York: Vienna House, 1974.

———. *Alban Berg: Leben und Werk*. Zurich: Atlantis, 1963.

———. "Alban Bergs neues Werk: 'Dem Andenken eines Engels.'" *Neues Wiener Journal*, August 31, 1935.

———. "Alban Bergs neuestes Werk." *Schweizerische Musikzeitung* 75, no. 23 (1935): 735–37.

———. "Ein Wiener Musiker übersetzt Mussolini." *Anbruch: Österreichische Zeitschrift für Musik* 17, no. 4 (1935): 107–9.

———. "Requiem für Manon." *Anbruch: Österreichische Zeitschrift für Musik* 17, no. 9 (1935): 250–52.

[Reich, Willi?]. "Alban Bergs Requiem für Manon." *Anbruch: Österreichische Zeitschrift für Musik* 18, no. 8 (1936): 233–34.

————. "Zur Entstehung des Violinkonzertes von Alban Berg." *Anbruch: Österreichische Zeitschrift für Musik* 18, no. 7 (1936): 196–97.

Reik, Theodor. *The Haunting Melody.* New York: Farrar, Straus and Young, 1953.

Rieger, Eva. *Friedelind Wagner: Richard Wagner's Rebellious Granddaughter.* Translated by Chris Walton. Woodbridge, England: Boydell & Brewer, 2013.

————. *"Leuchtende Liebe, lachender Tod": Richard Wagners Bild der Frau im Spiegel seiner Musik.* Düsseldorf: Patmos & Winkler, 2009.

Rihm, Wolfgang. *Ausgesprochen: Schriften und Gespräche.* 2 vols. Winterthur, Switzerland: Amadeus Verlag, 1997.

Rosé, Alfred. "Mahler und Hans von Bülow." In *Das Unterhaltungsblatt der Vossischen Zeitung* no. 286, published with the *Vossische Zeitung* no. 577, "Morgenausgabe," December 7, 1929.

Rose, Mike. *Writer's Block: The Cognitive Dimension.* Carbondale: Southern Illinois University Press, 2009.

Roth, Ernst. "Richard Strauss in London 1947." In *Richard Strauss Jahrbuch 1954,* edited by Willi Schuh, 132–40. Bonn: Boosey & Hawkes, 1953.

Rufer, Josef. *Das Werk Arnold Schönbergs.* Kassel: Bärenreiter, 1959.

Sartin, Jeffrey S. "Contagious Rhythm: Infectious Diseases of 20th Century Musicians." *Clinical Medicine & Research* 8, no. 2 (2010): 106–13.

Schaal, Susanne. "Abschied vom Leben oder musikpolitisches Manifest? Die *Vier letzten Lieder* von Richard Strauss." In vol. 2 of *Musik als Text: Bericht über den Internationalen Kongress der Gesellschaft für Musikforschung Freiburg im Breisgau 1993,* edited by Hermann Danuser and Tobias Plebuch, 548–51. Kassel: Bärenreiter, 1998.

Schabbing, Bernd. *Gustav Mahler als Konzert- und Operndirigent in Hamburg.* Berlin: Verlag Ernst Kuhn, 2002.

Schering, Arnold. "Geschichtliches zur 'ars inveniendi' in der Musik." In *Jahrbuch der Musikbibliothek Peters für 1925,* edited by Rudolf Schwartz, 25–34. Leipzig, Germany: C. F. Peters, 1926.

Schmitz, Eugen. Review of "Adagio" for orchestra, by Wilhelm Furtwängler. *Signale der musikalischen Welt* 64, no. 19/20 (March 7, 1906): 332.

Schoenberg, Arnold. "Composition with Twelve Tones." In *"Stile herrschen, Gedanken siegen": Ausgewählte Schriften,* edited by Anna Maria Morazzoni, 161–89. Mainz, Germany: Schott, 2007.

————. *Harmonielehre.* Vienna: Universal Edition, 1911.

————. *"Stile herrschen, Gedanken siegen": Ausgewählte Schriften.* Edited by Anna Maria Morazzoni. Mainz, Germany: Schott, 2007.

————. "Vortrag, zu halten in Frankfurt am Main am 12.II.1933." Edited by Thomas McGeary. *Journal of the Arnold Schoenberg Institute* 15, no. 2 (1992): 22–90.

Scholz, Gottfried. "More on Secret Programs." In *Encrypted Messages in Alban Berg's Music,* edited by Siglind Bruhn, 45–64. New York: Garland, 1998.

Schopenhauer, Arthur. "Versuch über das Geistersehn und was damit zusammenhängt." In vol. 1 of *Parerga und Paralipomena: Kleine philosophische Schriften*, 213–96. Berlin: Hayn, 1851.

———. *Die Welt als Wille und Vorstellung*. 2 vols. Leipzig, Germany: Reclam, 1890.

Schubert, Giselher. "'Vision' und 'Materialisation' zum Kompositionsprozess bei Hindemith." In *Vom Einfall zum Kunstwerk: Der Kompositionsprozess in der Musik des 20. Jahrhunderts*, edited by Hermann Danuser and Günter Katzenberger, 219–41. Laaber, Germany: Laaber-Verlag, 1993.

Schubert, Gotthilf Heinrich von. *Die Symbolik des Traumes*. Edited by Friedrich Heinrich Ranke. 4th ed. Leipzig, Germany: F. A. Brockhaus, 1862.

Schuh, Willi. "Richard Strauss's 'Four Last Songs.'" Translated by Max Loewenthal. *Tempo*, 2nd ser., no. 15 (1950): 25–27, 29–30.

———. "Strauss during the War Years." *Tempo*, no. 13 (1945): 8–10.

Schuhmann, Bruno. "Arthur Seidl: Ein Beitrag zum Problem der Künstlererziehung." In *Musik und Kultur: Festschrift zum 50. Geburtstag Arthur Seidl's*, edited by Bruno Schuhmann, 3–44. Regensburg: Bosse, 1913.

Schumann, Robert. "Hector Berlioz, Episode de la vie d'un artiste etc. (Schluss)." *Neue Zeitschrift für Musik* 3, nos. 13/14 (1835): 49–51.

Seidl, Arthur. *Moderner Geist in der deutschen Tonkunst: Vier Vorträge*. Berlin: Harmonie, 1900.

Seidl, Arthur, and Wilhelm Klatte. *Richard Strauss: Eine Charakterskizze*. Prague: O. Payer, 1896.

Shreffler, Anne C. "Ideologies of Serialism: Stravinsky's *Threni* and the Congress for Cultural Freedom." In *Music and the Aesthetics of Modernity: Essays*, edited by Karol Berger and Anthony Newcomb, 217–45. Cambridge, MA: Harvard University Department of Music, 2005.

Spalding, David. "You and I and Nobody Knows: Singing Our Dreams." *Canadian Folk Music Bulletin* 19, no. 4 (1985): 9–10.

Spitta, Philipp. *Joh. Seb. Bach*, vol. 2. Leipzig: Breitkopf & Härtel, 1921.

Stefan, Paul. *Gustav Mahler: Eine Studie über Persönlichkeit und Werk*. Munich: Piper, 1910.

Steiger, Martina. *"Immer wieder werden mich thätige Geister verlocken": Alma Mahler-Werfels Briefe an Alban Berg und seine Frau*. Vienna: Seifert, 2008.

Stephan, Rudolf. "Von der Planung zum musikalischen Kunstwerk." In *Vom Einfall zum Kunstwerk*, edited by Hermann Danuser and Günter Katzenberger, 253–72. Laaber, Germany: Laaber-Verlag, 1993.

Stockmann, Bernhard. "'Ruht wohl, ihr teuren Gebeine': Die Trauerfeiern für Hans von Bülow." In *Festschrift für Horst Gronemeyer zum 60. Geburtstag*, edited by Harald Weigel, 461–77. Herzberg: Traugott Bautz, 1993.

Strauss, Richard, *Betrachtungen und Erinnerungen*. Edited by Willi Schuh. Munich: Piper, 1989.

———. *Briefwechsel mit Willi Schuh*. Edited by Willi Schuh. Zurich: Atlantis, 1969.

———. "Erinnerungen an meinen Vater." In Strauss, *Betrachtungen und Erinnerungen*, 194–202.

———. "Künstlerisches Vermächtnis: An Dr. Karl Böhm." In Strauss, *Betrachtungen und Erinnerungen*, 69–75.

———. "Vom melodischen Einfall." In Strauss, *Betrachtungen und Erinnerungen*, 161–67.

Strauss, Richard, Igor Stravinsky, and Zoltan Kodály. "Correspondence with Dr. Roth." In *Tempo*, 2nd ser., no. 98 (1972): 9–20.

Stravinsky, Igor, and Robert Craft. *Conversations with Igor Stravinsky*. Berkeley: University of California Press, 1980.

———. *Expositions and Developments*. Berkeley: University of California Press, 1981.

Stresemann, Wolfgang. . . . *und abends in die Philharmonie: Erinnerungen an grosse Dirigenten*. Munich: Kristall bei Langen-Müller, 1981.

Sutcliffe, Tom. "Are We Still Backing the Wrong Horse?" *Independent*, September 17, 2010. http://www.independent.co.uk/voices/columnists/thomas-sutcliffe/tom-sutcliffe-are-we-still-backing-the-wrong-horse-2081193.html.

Taruskin, Richard. *The Danger of Music and Other Anti-utopian Essays*. Berkeley: University of California Press, 2009.

Tatlow, Ruth, and Paul Griffiths. "Numbers and Music." In *Grove Music Online*. Oxford University Press. Accessed July 2013.

Tenschert, Roland. "Richard Strauss' Schwanengesang: Vier letzte Lieder für Sopran und Orchester." In *Straussiana aus vier Jahrzehnten*. Tutzing: Schneider, 1994.

Thayer, Alexander Wheelock. *Ludwig van Beethovens Leben*. Vol. 1. Berlin: Ferdinand Schneider, 1866.

Trémine, René. *Wilhelm Furtwängler: Concert Listing 1906–1954*. Paris: Tahra Productions, 1997.

Trenner, Franz. *Richard Strauss: Chronik zu Leben und Werk*. Edited by Florian Trenner. Vienna: Verlag Dr. Richard Strauss, 2003.

Voss, Liselotte. *Die Entstehung von Thomas Manns Roman "Doktor Faustus."* Tübingen: Max Niemeyer, 1975.

Wagner, Cosima. *Die Tagebücher*. 2 vols. Munich: Piper, 1976–77.

Wagner, Friedelind, and Page Cooper. *Heritage of Fire: The Story of Richard Wagner's Granddaughter*. New York: Harper & Brothers, 1945.

Wagner, Richard. *Beethoven*. Leipzig, Germany: Fritzsch, 1870.

———. *Das braune Buch: Tagebuchaufzeichnungen, 1865 bis 1882*. Edited by Joachim Bergenfeld. Zurich: Atlantis Musikbuch-Verlag, 1975.

———. "Brief an einen italienischen Freund über die Aufführung des *Lohengrin* in Bologna." In vol. 9 of *Sämtliche Schriften und Dichtungen*, 341–45. Leipzig, Germany: Fritzsch, 1873.

———. *Mein Leben*. Edited by Martin Gregor-Dellin. Munich: List Verlag, 1977.

———. *Sämtliche Briefe*. Vol. 6. Edited by Hans-Joachim Bauer and Johannes Forner. Leipzig, Germany: Deutscher Verlag für Musik, 1986.

Walter, Bruno. *Thema und Variationen: Erinnerungen und Gedanken*. Frankfurt am Main: Fischer, 1963.

Walter Lindt, Lotte, ed. *Bruno Walter Briefe, 1894–1962*. Frankfurt am Main: Fischer, *1969*.

Walter, Mariko Namba, and Eva Jane Neumann Fridman, eds. *Shamanism: An Encyclopedia of World Beliefs, Practices, and Culture*. Vol. 1. Santa Barbara: ABC-CLIO, 2004.

Walton, Chris. *Othmar Schoeck und seine Zeitgenossen: Essays über Alban Berg, Ferruccio Busoni, Hermann Hesse, James Joyce, Thomas Mann, Max Reger, Igor Strawinsky und andere*. Winterthur, Switzerland: Amadeus Verlag, 2002.

———. *Richard Wagner's Zurich: The Muse of Place*. Rochester, NY: Camden House, 2007.

———. "Upstairs, Downstairs: Acoustics and Tempi in Wagner's 'Träume' and *Siegfried Idyll*." *Musical Times* 153, no. 1918 (2012): 7–18.

Zurlinden, Hans. "Einige Briefe von Richard Strauss aus seinen letzten Schweizerjahren." In *Erinnerungen*. St. Gallen, Switzerland: Tschudy-Verlag, 1962.

Zychowicz, James L. "'They Only Give Rise to Misunderstandings': Mahler's Sketches in Context." In *Genetic Criticism and the Creative Process: Essays from Music, Literature, and Theater*, edited by William Kinderman and Joseph E. Jones, 151–69. Rochester, NY: University of Rochester Press, 2009.

INDEX

Eastman Studies in Music

Ralph P. Locke, Senior Editor
Eastman School of Music

A complete list of titles in the Eastman Studies in Music series
may be found on our website, www.urpress.com.

Lies and Epiphanies offers case studies on the "inspiration" of five composers—Richard Wagner, Gustav Mahler, Wilhelm Furtwängler, Richard Strauss, and Alban Berg. Their own tales of their epiphanies played a determining role in the reception history of their works: the finale of Mahler's Second Symphony was supposedly born of a "lightning bolt" of inspiration at the funeral of Hans von Bülow, while Alban Berg's Violin Concerto was purportedly his direct response to the tragic early death of Alma Mahler's daughter.

Chris Walton looks behind these tales to explore instead the composer's dual role as author and self-commentator, laying bare the fissures and inconsistencies within these artists' testimonies and revealing how the putatively extrarational world of creative inspiration intersects with the highly rational world of money and politics. As Walton points out, the composer often imposes on the audience an interpretation of a work and its genesis that is as superficial as the score itself is not. This study seeks to show why.

Chris Walton teaches music history at the Basel University of Music in Switzerland. He is the author of *Othmar Schoeck: Life and Works* (University of Rochester Press, 2009) and *Richard Wagner's Zurich: The Muse of Place* (Camden House, 2007).

"Lies or epiphanies? Chris Walton offers a fascinating exploration of the stories his chosen composers—German Romantics from Wagner to Strauss—have told about inspiration. His conclusion is powerful, even moving, but no less important are his portraits of these still-looming figures."

—Paul Griffiths, author of *The Substance of Things Heard: Writings*

"Instead of the hagiography that often masquerades for music history, Walton offers a candid assessment of some of the major compositional personae of the nineteenth and twentieth centuries. If we are unsurprised to learn that Wagner lied about the sources of his inspiration in order to intensify the pseudo-religious aura of his work, we may be disappointed to discover that Berg was significantly more friendly to Austrofascism than has been generally recognized, or that Richard Strauss repeatedly reinvented himself to best profit from the ruling power—whether the Kaiser, Hitler, or the Americans. In this important book, Walton debunks the myths of inspiration invented by composers and their canonizers in the contexts of power and money."

—Timothy L. Jackson, Distinguished University Research Professor of Music, College of Music, University of North Texas